3

2.59 —

550 — sticks

110 — lbs. —

THE GOVERNMENT
AND POLITICS OF
EAST GERMANY

POLITICS EDITOR
W. A. ROBSON, B.Sc.(Econ.),
Ph.D., Ll.M.
*Professor Emeritus of Administration
in the University of London*

The Government
and Politics of
East Germany

KURT SONTHEIMER
*Professor of Political Science
University of Munich*

WILHELM BLEEK
*Lecturer in Political Science
University of Munich*

Translated from the German by
URSULA PRICE

HUTCHINSON
UNIVERSITY LIBRARY
LONDON

HUTCHINSON & CO. (Publishers) LTD
3 Fitzroy Square, London W1

London Melbourne Sydney Auckland
Wellington Johannesburg Cape Town
and agencies throughout the world

First published 1975

Set in Monotype Times
Printed in Great Britain by The Anchor Press Ltd
and bound by Wm Brendon & Son Ltd
both of Tiptree, Essex

ISBN 0 09 122020 3 (cased)
     0 09 122021 1 (paper)

Contents

Abbreviations

The five political parties in the GDR

SED Sozialistische Einheitspartei Deutschlands
Socialist Unity Party of Germany

DBD Demokratische Bauernpartei Deutschlands
Democratic Agricultural Workers' Party

CDU Christlich-Demokratische Union
Christian-Democratic Union

LDPD Liberal-Demokratische Partei Deutschlands
Liberal Democratic Party

NDPD National-Demokratische Partei Deutschlands
National Democratic Party

Giant organizations

FDGB Der Freie Deutsche Gewerkschaftsbund
Free German Association of Trades Unions

FDJ Freie Deutsche Jugend
Free German Youth Organization

DFD Demokratischer Frauenbund Deutschlands
Democratic Association of German Women

Preface

For Germany and the German people the bitterest and most momentous result of the Second World War which Hitler had unleashed was the division of Germany. Since 1949 two German states have existed side by side instead of the former German Republic: the Federal Republic of Germany and the German Democratic Republic. Moreover, the easternmost provinces of that former Republic had been taken from it and placed under Polish administration, while East Prussia (the region around Königsberg, now known as Kaliningrad) had been directly incorporated into Soviet Russia. Thus the division of Germany has become the starting point for what has been known since 1945 as 'the German question'. Today the German question is primarily concerned with the possible political unification of Germany. The polarization of world politics following the Second World War decided the question firmly in favour of a division of Germany, at least for the time being.

The fact that the German people did not want the division of their country and that many found it hard to accept the fact that they had lost the war certainly does not mean that they did not have a considerable share in what happened. Although it was impossible for the Germans to impose their will on the controlling powers in world politics during the post-war period, especially as there was no way of establishing a general consensus of opinion, Germany has, nevertheless, to bear a special responsibility for causing the Second World War—this cannot be overemphasized. The division of Germany is an indirect result of the defeat of Hitler's Germany. To this extent the recognition of the outcome of the Second World War—as regards both the political existence of the GDR and also the western frontiers of Poland which are part of the agreement concluded by the Federal Chancellor Willy Brandt with Soviet Russia and Poland—is a politically necessary action in line with the relaxation of tension between East and West.

The *détente* between East and West, as has been clearly shown during the last few years, is only possible in any event if it takes the *status quo* at the end of the war as its starting point. The two German states belong to different spheres of power in world politics and are firmly rooted in them ideologically, economically and militarily in either case.

As a result of these developments, a change is now taking place in the political and academic interest of the Federal Republic in the other part of Germany. Over twenty years after the establishment of the German Democratic Republic, attention is no longer directed primarily at its dependence on the Soviet Union, nor even exclusively at its—from a western standpoint—anti-liberal and totalitarian characteristics. Today we are interested in the GDR as a political structure of individual stamp which, despite its general agreement with the Communist and totalitarian system of the Soviet Union, nevertheless possesses its own individuality and identity.

Clearer historical insight and the new political pattern of the East–West relationship have given rise to a tendency to come to terms with the GDR as a political and social entity of a special kind; this tendency has also become visible on all sides in western academic writing and journalism during the last few years. For this reason it is more than ever justifiable today to attempt a political, economic and social account of the GDR as this book intends to do. For today this second German state has a profile of its own: it is no longer simply an appendage of Soviet power and it possesses an economic weight of its own which has achieved for it some measure of manoeuvrability in its political relationships within the eastern bloc. More important still: the GDR has become acutely aware of its historical role and function as the first socialist state on German territory. This official view has not been adopted by everyone in the GDR, but it has at least contributed to the growth of a special political and social awareness amongst the East German people. Now, almost twenty-five years after the establishment of the state, most citizens accept the identification with the Communist régime in the GDR more as a matter of course and with more self-assurance than in its difficult early days. To the observer abroad the GDR presents itself today as a political entity in its own right. The German Democratic Republic is no longer a Soviet Zone of Occupation—

no less than the Federal Republic itself it represents both German history and present-day Germany.

Serious observers in the Federal Republic and other western countries who are studying conditions in the GDR realize that they are no longer dealing with a political entity, whose individual character can be sufficiently understood by using a simple static model of totalitarianism. Nevertheless, with the GDR any scientific study, hoping to avoid superficial and negative interpretations, is faced with a number of serious problems which were present from the very start. Students from western countries —and the Federal Republic in particular—have been allowed into the GDR only in exceptional cases. For their sources they have therefore had to depend primarily on material published in the GDR and have been unable to gather their own data or make their own enquiries. Furthermore, there is no doubt that the official image of itself which the GDR presents to the world corresponds far less with political and social realities than is the case with most western democracies. Nevertheless, it is important to try to form a realistic picture on the basis of the material available, for it is not possible to make one's own investigations.

This book cannot claim to present new research findings, but rather undertakes the hitherto unattempted task of giving a total picture of the political, social and economic system of the GDR together with its foreign policy. Since the available material constantly needs to be interpreted, value judgements are unavoidable. However, the authors of this book do not proceed from set assumptions about the superiority of the western system, nor do they set out to prove that the GDR is better than public opinion in the Federal Republic and in the western world generally would like to admit .The aim is first of all to give a coherent picture of the political system of the GDR in its entirety, and to show how it works and what problems it faces. It will be necessary both to take account of the special nature and relative independence of the GDR as the first socialist state on German soil and to analyse the claims which the GDR makes for itself and which must be examined in the light of ascertainable facts.

In the limited space available such an account cannot, of course, be exhaustive. It must concentrate on whatever appears to be most important. A coherent analysis of the most significant aspects of the GDR which seeks to explain the nature of the 'other' Germany even to the politically uninformed reader has now become an important element in education and the dissemination of political information. This is all the more necessary, because the GDR has meanwhile established regular connections with almost all countries in the world and has been officially accepted as a member of UNO.

The authors are both citizens of the Federal Republic. It is therefore impossible for them to deny their particular attitude to the other part of Germany which motivated this study. Nevertheless, they hope that this book will enable non-German readers, too, to gain a clearer picture of the assumptions and realities of the political system of East Germany.

Munich   Kurt Sontheimer
January 1974   Wilhelm Bleek

1 | The division of Germany and the birth of the GDR

In the political terminology of the GDR and the countries of the eastern bloc, the course of events between 1945 and 1949 leading to the establishment of two separate German states (in the West and in the East) is consistently referred to as the 'severance' of Germany. Western historians and politicians prefer to speak of 'division', which is less dynamic and seems to suggest an apparently inevitable historical development, rather than the active responsibility of people and powers. It thus expresses a significant difference in the historical evaluation of events which led up to the ending of German unity.

Because of these widely differing interpretations, it seems advisable to attempt a brief description of the historical events which led to the breakdown of four-power control over Germany, instituted by the Allied Control Commission. As will be seen, it reveals an international conflict of interests which could not be resolved by agreement but only by mutual limitation.

At the Yalta Conference in February 1945, Stalin, Churchill and Roosevelt had agreed, as the communiqué put it, on 'common guidelines and plans for the treatment of Germany' after the total defeat of the Hitler régime. The central part of this agreement was the temporary division of Germany into zones of occupation and the taking over of supreme power in Germany by the allied governments.

The division of Germany into first three, later four zones of occupation (due to France joining the other allies after the Yalta Conference) took place in accordance with the plan, which had been worked out as early as 1944 by the European Advisory Commission, set up by the heads of the three governments.

Neither at Yalta nor at this particular moment did the allies have any clear idea as to the concrete form that Germany was to take in the future. The Americans and the British debated various plans for splitting Germany up into several states in which Stalin showed some interest, but to which he never gave any long-term support. On 9 May 1945, the day after the capitulation of the German Army, Stalin declared that the Soviet Union intended neither to split up nor to destroy Germany. This made it clear that the Soviet Union, after separating the eastern territories beyond the Oder–Neisse line, was interested first of all in preserving the unity of Germany. The reason for this was that the Soviet Union, because of the enormous losses sustained during the war, attached much importance to the question of reparation and believed that a favourable outcome could only be achieved if Germany were treated as a whole and remained subject to the united power of the victors. Thus it came about that after the fruitless discussion of innumerable plans for splitting Germany up, the provisions of the Potsdam Agreement of 1945 once again placed the emphasis even more strongly on the unity of Germany. True, the division into zones still remained, but several points already provided for a uniform treatment of Germany as a whole.

The Allied Control Commission, consisting of the four commanders-in-chief of the allied forces in the zones of occupation, had been established to deal with all common matters affecting the whole of Germany. The efficient functioning and political weight of this Control Commission depended entirely on the extent to which the four powers could agree on uniform guidelines regarding the treatment of Germany. This was certainly true at the beginning. Of no less importance, however, was the question as to how such guidelines were to be followed in the individual zones. Since the Control Commission had no executive of its own, the carrying out of its decisions rested solely with the individual zone commanders; their differing interpretations of the Control Commission laws and their varying applications led in specific cases to considerable deviations from a uniform policy of occupation.

At Potsdam the allies had admittedly decided that for the time being no central German government should be formed; however, they wished to set up at least 'a few important central

German administrative departments', namely for finance, transport and traffic, as well as for foreign trade and industry. This plan was prevented by the objections of the French, who were on no account prepared to promote the creation of a central German government, unless their own claims to the annexation of the Saar and to participation in control of the Ruhr were met. The establishment of central German administrative offices in these fields might possibly have become the starting point for a uniform German administration under allied control. It would then also have provided the Control Council with the body which it was really intended to control.

The predominance of each individual occupying power within its own zone undermined even those decisions of the Potsdam Agreement which were meant to preserve at least the economic unity of Germany and ensure 'equality of treatment for the German population' by the military governments. In practice, each military governor ruled his zone as he thought best since, in many cases, no uniformity could be achieved owing to the right of veto in the Control Council. Furthermore, each one carried out many of the common measures decided in Potsdam (as for instance the de-Nazification and demilitarization of Germany) according to sometimes very differing conceptions. Even the intention of preparing 'the reconstruction of German political life on a democratic basis' was, in effect, anything but uniform. Bearing in mind the differences in American and Russian political ideas, bearing in mind also the different interests of the individual occupying powers with regard to the part of Germany they were ruling, it is not surprising that even where uniform decisions of the Control Council existed, their application led to vastly differing results.

The principle, clearly defined at Potsdam, of treating the whole of Germany as an economic unit regardless of its division into zones, was already broken at Potsdam itself in one important respect, which was soon to prove a decisive factor in the growing tension between the Soviet Union and the western powers and in the division of Germany arising from it. An understanding had been reached at Yalta concerning the reparations to be made by Germany. These, not surprisingly, were of particular importance to the Soviet Union. In dealing with them, however, the Potsdam Agreement had given up the principle of the economic unity of Germany by introducing a distinction between reparations from the eastern zone and those from the western zones. As had been agreed, the Soviet Union was to satisfy its demands for reparation out of the eastern zone, whilst the claims of the USA, England and France, together with all other countries entitled to compensation were to be met from the 'western zones' (as the Potsdam Agreement already puts it). Over and above this, the western powers declared themselves ready to yield to the Russians 25% of such industrial equipment of the western zones as was not necessary for a future German peace-time economy. This was intended to act as a kind of balancing factor in favour of the Russians, since the share of their zone in the total industrial capacity of Germany was very small. However, the Russians were to provide foodstuffs and other goods from their zone in return for 15 of this 25%.

It was this question of a 'return' which inflamed the conflict between East and West in the four-power control of Germany. Increasingly it paralysed the activities of the Control Council, and, together with the fusing of the western zones and the beginnings of a West German state, it finally led to the breakdown of four-power control altogether. As early as May 1946 the American Military Governor, General Clay, abruptly stopped supplies from the West to the Russians as 'reparation' because they had not honoured their obligation to supply foodstuffs and were taking their own reparation from the current production of the eastern zone. Yet this measure was symptomatic of the increasing estrangement between the allies rather than its cause. The main cause of the disagreement regarding the treatment of Germany as an economic unit was the growing incompatibility of the Russian and the British-American standpoints as to the advisability of carrying out extensive industrial dismantling and taking reparations in a ravaged country, whose people themselves did not have enough to live on.

It was the economic plight of Germany in particular which persuaded the Americans and the British in 1947 to stop their policy of dismantling and to fuse their two zones into a 'bizone', later to be joined also by the French zone. In addition, Germany was to be included in the programme of extensive economic aid, intended for the whole of Europe under the Marshall Plan. The innumerable conferences between the four Foreign Ministers

between 1945 and 1949, in which they vainly attempted to overcome the increasing differences of policy, especially with regard
to Germany, were unable to check the threatened separation
between the western zones and the eastern one, even had they
seriously wished to do so. Even the sessions of the Allied Control
Commission, meeting in Berlin, became more and more futile. It
therefore came as no great surprise when the Commander of
the Russian zone, Marshal Sokolowski, left the Control Council
building in Berlin on 20 March 1948 as a protest, after his western
colleagues had failed to give him information about decisions
made at the recently held conference of the western powers in
London, for which he had asked. These decisions dealt with the
formation of a West German state, the later Federal Republic.
With the Russian departure from the Control Council, the joint
four-power government of Germany had finally broken down.

. In answer to this new situation and following the introduction
of the new West German currency even into West Berlin, the
Russians began their blockade of Berlin. By this they hoped to
achieve control of the western sectors of the city by starving them
out, and to exert pressure on the western powers, to prevent
them setting up a West German 'separate state'. In the end this
attempt on West Berlin failed, thanks to the air-lift and the
determination of the West Berliners to preserve their freedom.
The Soviet Union finally gave in and agreed to lift the blockade
on condition that a conference of all the Foreign Ministers should
be summoned in Paris before the founding of the West German
state. At this four-power conference in Paris in May 1949 the
Russians made their last attempt to maintain a united Germany
under four-power control. Their demands for a return to the
Potsdam Agreement were linked with a suggested Peace Treaty,
to be concluded with an all-German 'State Council'; all four
occupying powers were to leave Germany one year after it had
been ratified.

At this point in time the western powers showed not the least
interest in the Soviet proposals for a return to German unity.
They were already so firmly committed to the idea of establishing
a West German state that they made the wholly unacceptable
suggestion to the Soviet Foreign Minister that the Soviet zone
should come within the jurisdiction of the Basic Law, about
to be passed in Bonn. In the year in which NATO came into

being, the military interest of the western powers, particularly the Americans, in the inclusion of Germany in a western defence community against the eastern bloc was already so strong that this final attempt at a four-power agreement had inevitably to fail and to lead to the creation of two completely separate German states.

The reasons which brought about the collapse of the Potsdam plan for a united Germany—planned at first only on an economic basis but intended to be followed by the restoration of its political unity—must be sought both in the division of Germany into four separate zones which posed major problems of organization to any common policy of occupation, as well as in the increasingly irreconcilable differences necessarily arising out of the distinct political systems of East and West. These differences prevented the realization of any viable common plan for treating Germany as an entity, and at the same time led to varying policies of occupation in the individual zones, which found expression on political, social, economic and cultural levels. In view of the divergent aims and methods, and the actual formulation of the Potsdam Agreement, it is indeed surprising that during the first few years of occupation a minimum of uniformity was in fact achieved.

Against the background of these almost irreconcilable interests, which could not be ignored—despite premature American hopes for creating an era of lasting world peace—the particular causes which brought about the division of Germany between 1946 and 1947 are, if anything, of secondary importance. They only served to underline the fundamental conflict of interests between the major powers, which could equally easily have manifested itself elsewhere, such as in the question of reparations.

Nevertheless, the occupying powers (apart from France) did not originally want a division of Germany. In allowing France to join them as agreed at Yalta, however, they had failed to make it a condition that France should be bound by the Potsdam Agreement. Thus from the very beginning de Gaulle and Bidault were able both to stand apart from the Potsdam Agreement and to prevent it from being put into practice, because France had not been signatory to it. It is possible that the setting up of central German administrative offices, blocked by the French, might have formed the basis of a new unified German state, even in spite of its division into zones. On the other hand, it seems likely that the conflicts which finally led to the collapse of German unity would also have appeared within such a framework. The division of Germany was both an effect of the political polarization of the USA and the Soviet Union, as well as one of its causes. And by 1947–8, with the Marshall Plan and the separate currency reform, the division of Germany would in any case have become inevitable.

Regarding the historically interesting question as to whether the West or the East had a greater share in bringing about the division of Germany, the Soviet Union and the East German side appear to have the better documentary evidence in their favour. The Russians had obstinately clung to the Potsdam plan for maintaining German unity because in this way they hoped to exert additional influence on the western part of Germany not controlled by themselves. In repeated notes to the western powers, they protested against the increasingly real project of establishing a West German state under western control, because they rightly saw it as a threat to the interests of the Soviet Union in central Europe. Only after the western powers had taken all steps within their own spheres of influence towards making the two parts of Germany independent, did the Soviet Union do so in theirs. The currency reform in the western zone and West Berlin preceded currency reform in the eastern zone; the passing of the Basic Law by parliament in the Federal Republic preceded by one week the legitimation of the draft constitution of the GDR by the People's Congress; a few weeks after the setting up of the constitutional organs of the new Federal Republic in September 1949 there followed on 7 October the founding of the German Democratic Republic. Seen from the standpoint of the Soviet Union and the GDR the responsibility for the division of Germany therefore lies clearly with the western powers and the West Germans.

This interpretation by the East is correct in so far as the Russians and also the representatives of German politics in the Soviet Union repeated their theme of unity and their desire to uphold the Potsdam Agreement almost *ad nauseam*. At the same time, however, they made it clear both in their speeches and not least, more concretely in their actual transformation of the Soviet zone into an 'anti-Fascist democratic' state ruled by the working classes, that they saw 'democracy' as being a preliminary stage towards a socialist democracy of the Soviet type and not as a free democratic basis for a liberal constitutional state with a capitalist economic structure in the western sense.

Those who explain the rise of Fascism from the socio-economic form of capitalism, as do the Communists, must also of course dispose of the socio-economic basic conditions of the capitalist system, in which 'exploitation' does not exist. This is the reason behind the GDR's boast that she alone conscientiously fulfilled all conditions of the Potsdam Agreement. 'Militarism, Imperialism and Nazism are rooted out, war criminals have been punished and removed from all official posts.'[1]

It is certainly true that the terms of the Potsdam Agreement, which required the elimination of National Socialism and its causes, were complied with more thoroughly and effectively in the Soviet zone of occupation than in the western zones. However, the Russians could surely not have expected that the Americans and the British would renounce their belief in civil rights and a free economy nor that they would deprive the German people of all power in favour of a Communist-inspired government by the working classes. There was nothing to suggest that the western occupying powers would consider the personal ownership of production equipment to be a source of anti-democratic ideas and would therefore abolish it. Conversely, the upheaval of social and political conditions in the Soviet zone which was carried out with such determination as to make them, one by one, resemble those under Soviet rule, was bound to provoke opposition to the Soviet ideas for a unified Germany amongst the western powers generally and the West Germans in particular.

When political systems, based on different ethical and structural principles, possess a common object in their search for power and each seeks to transform it according to these principles, a growing conflict between them must, sooner or later, become inevitable. Today one solution for such conflicts of power is that of partition, which has been tried not only in Germany but also in Asia (Korea, Vietnam). In spite of the anti-Hitler coalition, the basic requirements for a common policy towards Germany did not exist amongst the victorious powers, unless indeed they had been prepared to leave a conquered Germany entirely to its own devices. Yet none of the allies who had parti-

---

[1] Superior figures refer to end-of-chapter notes.

cipated in the major war against Hitler could have had any interest in such a step. Thus, in face of the polarized balance of power and with the political aims of the former allies becoming increasingly irreconcilable, the almost inevitable result came about—the division of Germany. 'The division of Germany . . . is the result of the transformation of the continent of Europe into a power vacuum, following Hitler's war and defeat, thereby causing a powerless Europe to be rent apart into two power-blocks under the leadership of the USA and the USSR, both being super-powers on the fringes of Europe. To this extent it is not the direct but most probably the indirect consequence of the disaster brought upon Europe by the Third Reich.'[2]

2 THE SOVIET POLICY OF OCCUPATION

By its victory over Hitler's army the Soviet Union had, for the first time in its history, penetrated deep into central Europe. The Soviet military rule over Poland, Czechoslovakia and most of the Balkan countries, created the essential requirement for a thorough transformation of the inner balance of power within the countries liberated and occupied by the Red Army. It was quite clear that the Russians would not relinquish control of that zone of Germany entrusted to them, whatever might happen to Germany as a whole. In the course of safeguarding their newly-won territories, the Russians were more concerned with establishing their zone as a secure outpost of Soviet power in central Europe, than with searching with the western powers for a common policy towards Germany. Nevertheless, the theme of a united Germany in the light of Potsdam gave them a good propagandist tune at a time when the western powers were seeking separate solutions for Germany in order to master the problems of rebuilding their zones. The division of Germany foreshadowed an intensification in the division of Europe, symbolized by the iron curtain, which has split Europe ever since. The final drop of this curtain took place when the Soviet Union refused to accept American aid through the Marshall Plan for the states within its own control.

In individual cases the Soviet policy of occupation could also refer back to decisions made at Potsdam, which had as their declared aim 'the final restructuring of German political life

on a democratic basis'. It was not surprising that the practical
effects of this decision in the Soviet zone differed from those of
the three western zones. Admittedly the Russians did not pursue
a strict course of 'sovietization' in their zone from the outset,
but in the long term it was, as already mentioned, the aim of the
Soviet occupying power to create such conditions in the zone
under their control as would correspond ideologically, economically and in their organization of state and community to the
Soviet model of a socialist democracy. As the tensions with the
western powers grew stronger and their intention—given first
economic and then military motivation—to pursue their own
path in recreating a civil democracy in their zones and finally
to set up a West German state became clearer, so too did the
Russians pursue their aim more consistently. This aim was fully
realized in the stage after the establishment of the GDR.

Besides the question of reparations, the Soviet Union's first
concern after the war was to destroy all remnants of German
Nazism and militarism (including its rearmament potential)
so that Germany could never again become a dangerous threat
to peace. In this aim the western powers were at first in agreement with the Russians in principle (as is shown, for instance,
by the absurd American Morgenthau Plan), but the concrete
application of the Potsdam decisions soon led to the differences
described above. These became mutually unbridgeable at the
precise moment when the Soviet Union realized that America
was carrying out a gradual incorporation of the West German
zones into the economic and military organization of the West,
thus causing the larger and potentially more powerful part of
Germany to become once again a threat to the Soviet Union.
In the eyes of the Russians the essential purpose of the anti-
Hitler coalition had thus been betrayed. Therefore the complete
incorporation of what later became the GDR into the economic
and defence framework of the eastern bloc led by the Soviet
Union was no more than a logical and consistent answer to the
policy of the western allies.

Reparations and inner upheavals

To ensure that its claims for compensation would be met, the
Soviet Union dismantled more than 1000 firms wholly or in

part and transported them to the East. A further 200 firms which were on the list for intended dismantling were converted into Soviet Limited Companies and their production was thenceforth credited to the Soviet account. The share of these companies in the total production of the Soviet zone of occupation after 1945 is estimated at approximately 25%.

Under such conditions it was particularly difficult for the newly-formed German authorities to get the economic life in their zones going again: the agricultural production of foodstuffs too was not sufficient to supply even the most urgent needs, especially as the occupying power also expected to draw supplies from the land. Politically it was an obvious step to combine increasing agricultural production with extensive agrarian reform. This agrarian reform was planned in detail by the Soviet military administration and begun as early as the end of 1945. In the main, it was in accordance with the intentions of the two socialist parties, the KPD and the SPD. Even the more right-wing parties had not argued in favour of retaining the large estates east of the Elbe.

All landowners who possessed more than a hundred hectares of land were expropriated. The whole of these estates, together with the land already belonging to the state and that of former Nazi leaders were put into a central pool, out of which about half a million people, both resettlers as well as agricultural workers and smallholders were supplied with new property. It was not always possible at that time to create viable agricultural units, so that this agrarian reform was, at the same time, a preparation for the idea of collective farming, begun a few years later.

Just as drastic as the agrarian reform was the reform of industry. Following a decree by the military administration, all the industrial property belonging to the German state, the National Socialist Party and its allied organizations was confiscated. Those firms concerned, which were not immediately turned into Soviet Limited Companies, were put at the disposal of the newly-formed German authorities. Moreover, all firms whose owners or directors had fled were nationalized. By these methods, the greater part of all industries was seized and appropriated. In Saxony a relatively free referendum on 30 June 1946 sanctioned the 'appropriation of property belonging to war criminals' thereby removing a large part of industry from private ownership.

Other drastic reforms were concerned with education and justice. The reform of education proclaimed the creation of a unified educational system and the abolition of all private schooling. A common school system has existed in East Germany since 1946, with eight years elementary schooling for everyone, followed by higher school or vocational training. The reform of justice provided for total de-Nazification; any judge or member of the state legal service who had been a member of the Nazi party was barred from employment. This affected more than four fifths of them. They were replaced by politically reliable persons known as 'people's judges' who were trained for their new work in special short courses.

All in all, these 'reforms' brought about a very thorough transformation of social and economic conditions in the eastern zone of Germany, which differed markedly from developments in West Germany. Nevertheless, these measures could also be interpreted as being derived from the Potsdam decisions, for it would have been unrealistic to expect that the Soviet Union would attach the same meaning to the concepts 'democracy' and 'reconstruction of democracy' in Germany as their allied partners in the West. Especially if the blame for the war and the rise of Nazism and militarism were attributed to the economic forces of capitalism, it would not be sufficient, according to a communist standpoint, merely to control them more strongly or to limit them; rather, it would be necessary to remove them for good. In any event, it was essential to ensure that the setting up of a democracy was also anti-Fascist; in communist terms this could only mean that the middle classes who had contributed so greatly to the rise of Fascism should have no further opportunity to bring any influence to bear on the process of democratization. Since the more right-wing parties, which were anxious to regain some share of political responsibility, were prepared after the war to agree to an anti-Fascist programme, the Soviet occupying power was ready to let them co-operate in a 'block of anti-Fascist democratic parties', particularly as this would provide, for a time, a façade of bourgeois democracy.

The formation of political parties in the eastern zone

Although, immediately after their defeat, the Germans were debarred from any political activity of their own, the Soviet military government in Germany rather surprisingly issued the following decree on 10 June 1945, only one day after its formation: 'Within the territories of the Soviet zone of occupation in Germany the formation and activity of all such anti-Fascist parties may be permitted, which have as their aim the final eradication of all remnants of Fascism, the strengthening of the bases of democracy and civil rights in Germany and the development of initiative and self-sufficiency amongst the mass of the people towards this end.' This decree came as a surprise to the western powers because they had planned to allow the formation of political parties only after some time had passed and then only at a local level. It even came as a surprise to the German Communists who were originally meant to concentrate solely on filling posts in the German administration with suitable candidates and did not expect to be able to form a political party at so early a stage.

As early as 30 April a group of ten German Communists under the leadership of Walter Ulbricht had flown from Moscow to Frankfurt an der Oder to support the Red Army in setting up a German administration. This group, which immediately began its work in the headquarters of the Soviet Army, had, as Walter Ulbricht has reported, been 'well prepared', that is, it had concrete plans for the reorganization of the German administration under Soviet occupation. The first task it dealt with was the setting up of administrative districts in Berlin for which, first of all, suitable candidates had to be found. For this it was considered important to put forward not only Communists but also trustworthy non-Communists so that the suspicion of a Communist seizure of power should not arise.

Even the Communist Party itself, holding its foundation conference on 11 June one day after the second Soviet decree, spoke in its first manifesto against the immediate introduction of the Soviet system and demanded instead the setting up of an anti-Fascist democratic régime, in which all political parties were to work together. The Communist reason for propounding this view—namely that it would be wrong to impose the Soviet system on Germany—arose on the one hand out of the political consideration that the immediate transformation of Germany into a Soviet-type state would not only arouse strong internal opposition but would also endanger co-operation with the western allies regarding Germany as a whole. On the other hand there was the theoretical consideration that it was necessary first to bring to an end the democratic restructuring of Germany, first begun in 1848, and to abolish all remnants of feudalism, before attempting the first steps towards a socialist state. Only after the introduction of a parliamentary democracy would the way be clear for a socialist democracy. This early anti-Fascist democratic stage under the protection of Soviet occupation is thus seen by the GDR as a necessary preliminary to the development of a socialist democracy led by a Unity Party of the working classes.

The first public appearance of the Communist Party of Germany (KPD) led by Wilhelm Pieck was followed a few days later by the foundation manifesto of the Socialist Party (SPD) under the leadership of Otto Grotewohl. Previously a few Social Democrats had attempted, in discussions with the Communists, to set up a United German Workers' Party, but at this stage the KPD were not yet thinking of a Socialist Unity Party. They wanted first of all to build up their own core organization in order to bring about an alliance on a more firmly organized and ideological basis at a later date if the occasion arose.

At the end of June the CDU was formed as a third party, with a programme which accepted the idea of private ownership in so far as it did not conflict with responsibility towards the community in general; beyond this it underlined its proclaimed principles of Christian Socialism by requiring that mineral resources, mining and other monopolistic key industries of the economy should be 'subject to the power of the state'. Most strongly rooted in the old bourgeois tradition was the programme of the Liberal Democratic Party which stood for private ownership, a free economy and the independence of the judiciary and civil servants.

All four parties, whose leading members were, in the main, recruited from the corresponding parties of the Weimar Republic, were active throughout the whole of the east zone and joined together after only a few weeks (on 14 July) to form the 'block of anti-Fascist democratic parties'. A committee was formed consisting of five members from each of the four parties to discuss and agree a common policy. This principle of agreement guaranteed a majority for the Communists who were in league with the ruling occupying power. Indeed, during this early stage, everything depended on finding out and knowing exactly what the occupying power considered to be right and acceptable. Thanks to the close alliance between the Communist Party and the Soviet military administration, thanks also to the principle of block voting on agreed policies, the three remaining parties could not hope to assert themselves against the Communist Party and Soviet-directed policies.

The beginnings of the SED

The co-operation between the two workers' parties on the basis of organizational independence lasted for only a short time. During the last months of 1945, the KPD suddenly pressed for an amalgamation which it had previously refused. Poor results for the Communists at the first post-war elections in Austria must certainly have contributed to the new strategy of enforced integration. The SPD leadership of the east zone was no longer as interested in the formation of a united workers' party as it had been immediately after the end of the war, not only on account of some unfortunate experiences in its agreed co-operation with the KPD, but also because it saw how the KPD was continually favoured by the Soviet occupying power. The chairman of the SPD in the West, Dr Kurt Schumacher, had from the outset been a determined opponent of amalgamation, and attempted to exert some influence to this end on his colleagues in the East. But actual conditions proved stronger than doubts. In the discussions on amalgamation between the leading groups, the KPD cleverly made a few formal concessions. The occupying power, on its part, forcibly brought an amalgamation about by coercive measures against its opponents. In particular it exerted pressure on local party organizations which, in many places, had already joined together even before the amalgamation was officially ratified at a joint party conference. Furthermore the SPD was divided on this issue. After the Communists had declared themselves ready to agree to the remarkable thesis of a 'special German way towards Socialism', opposition to the amalgamation finally disappeared, even amongst those leaders of the Social Democrats in the East who, in any case, saw only few effective opportunities for opposition to the proposed amalgamation. The Berlin Social-Democrats alone, supported in the western part of the city by the western powers, took a referendum amongst their members on the question of amalgamation, which showed an overwhelming majority of 82% to be against it.

The joint party conference at which the Socialist Unity Party *Sozialistische Einheitspartei Deutschlands* (SED) came into being, took place on 21 and 22 April 1946. The executive of the new party was composed equally of Social Democrats and Communists: Wilhelm Pieck of the KPD and Otto Grotewohl of the SPD were appointed as joint chairmen. The handshake of the two party leaders became the symbolic expression of their unity and adorns the emblem of the SED.

Historians of the GDR praise the establishment of the SED as being 'the greatest achievement in the history of the German workers' movement since the publication of the Communist Manifesto'.[3] But already in 1947 only one year after the amalgamation, the transformation of the party into a 'new-type' party began. This was the development towards a 'closed Marxist-Leninist party, both ideologically and in political organization'. Under the existing conditions the Social Democrats could only be the losers in such an amalgamation. With this new party, the SED, representing the unity of the working classes, the Communists went forward confidently to the first elections.

First elections

The first local elections took place in the east zone in September 1946. They resulted in the new Unity Party obtaining slightly more than 50% of the votes, which however, was less than the party leadership had expected. The SED also won the district and *Land* elections, held for the first time shortly afterwards (on 20 October 1946), but its share of the vote in all five *Länder* was actually below 50%. This admittedly enabled them to appoint their own members to key posts in the five *Land* governments particularly in the Ministries of the Interior and of Culture. It was clear to them, however, that it was certainly not possible to speak of a majority of the working-class party in these relatively free elections. Of special interest for a probable distribution of votes by the electors of East Germany in really free elections and without the compulsory amalgamation of the SPD with the KPD were the elections also held on 20 October in Greater Berlin. There the SPD gained 48·7% of the votes, the SED only 19·8%. Taken together these gave a clear majority to the two workers' parties, but it was an unmistakable indication of the Berlin electors' rejection of the KPD in favour of the Social Democrats.

Thanks to the amalgamation, however, the SPD no longer presented any real problem to the KPD which had the protection of the occupying power in its zone. The way towards the development of the SED as a Communist Party in close association with the party of the Soviet Union and based on the doctrines of Marx, Lenin and Stalin, now lay open. It was followed through to its logical conclusion at the second Party Conference by the end of which there emerged a Communist Party of Soviet stamp, which no longer contained any noticeable elements of Social Democratic principles.

In its dealings with the originally more right-wing parties the SED has continued its method of block voting until today. To weaken the right-wing forces which were not so easily neutralized, two further parties were founded in 1948 with the approval of the military authorities, the National Democratic Party of Germany (NDPD) and the Democratic Agricultural Workers' Party of Germany, *Demokratische Bauernpartei Deutschlands* (DBD). The CDU and Liberal Democrats increasingly forfeited their relative independence and could no longer develop individual programmes under the rule of the growing and Communist-led SED. The block vote was supplemented even further by the inclusion of such giant organizations as the trade unions, which had been ruled by the Communists from the beginning, together with the Democratic League of Women and the Free German Youth Movement. This completed the formation of the National Front, the union of all political parties and giant organizations which was officially called into being on 4 October 1949 under the leadership of the SED.

3 THROUGH 'UNITY' TOWARDS SEPARATION

The SED and those political groups allied with it in an anti-Fascist block ceaselessly emphasized the idea of a united German state. They accused the western powers and the Germans working with them of dividing the country and disregarding the Potsdam decisions. In order to demonstrate their intention of restoring German unity, several People's Congresses were organized, in which a number of mainly Communist delegates from the western zones also took part. The first of these People's Congresses for Freedom and Unity took place at the end of 1947 and the second only three months later!

From the second congress there emerged a German People's Council which claimed to have the right to represent the German people and set up a committee which was to work out guidelines for the constitution of a German Democratic Republic concerned with the whole of Germany, parallel to the deliberations of the Parliamentary Council in Bonn. The constitution later accepted by the third People's Congress in May 1949 corresponded largely to a draft originally considered by the SED in 1946. In this constitution, too, the idea of a whole Germany was retained, even though it was obvious that it would only apply to the eastern parts of the state. Thus Article 1 proclaimed: 'Germany is an indivisible democratic republic'.

This propaganda in favour of German unity by the SED, its allied partners and the giant organizations was made all the easier for the politicians because the West saw every attempt by the Soviet occupying power and the SED to restore German unity as an attempt to expand Communist influence on German territory and therefore blocked it.

To this extent the GDR can point to a fairly continuous endeavour in its attitudes and policies to restore German unity on the basis of the Potsdam decisions. Furthermore the Soviet and East German politicians were at great pains to see that all the actual steps leading to the division of the country were first taken by the western powers, who would therefore have to take responsibility for them. At the beginning of October 1949, the Soviet Union promptly protested against the formation of a

West German government, and informed the western powers whom they held responsible for the division of Germany 'that a new situation had arisen as a result of the existence of a separate German government in Bonn'. This new situation led shortly afterwards to the well-prepared establishment of the German Democratic Republic as the second German state. On 7 October 1949 the German People's Council proclaimed the new republic, ratified the creation of a provisional parliament and a provisional government and immediately constituted itself into a People's Chamber under the terms of the new GDR constitution. Elections for the newly created People's Assembly were not to take place until a year later.

The Federal German government under Chancellor Adenauer declared the new German state illegitimate, since the electors in the Soviet zone had not been allowed to express their political views freely. In accordance with the Basic Law of the Federal Republic, Adenauer claimed to be the sole representative of the interests of all the German people. The GDR could therefore have no right to speak on questions concerning Germany as a whole. Speaking for the GDR, the new Minister President Grotewohl declared that his government had been given its mandate by the people and was, in fact, the first independent German government.

The official history of the GDR describes the establishment of that state as the visible culmination of the anti-Fascist democratic upheaval. The GDR is seen as the 'first truly democratic, peaceloving German state . . . in which power is given to the working classes and their colleagues, such as farm labourers and other democratic sections of society'.[4] Claims for unity, national rebirth and reunification were also made in the GDR from the beginning for, according to the official version, 'the basis for the national rebirth of Germany as a peaceloving and democratic state arose in October 1949 in the shape of the German Democratic Republic'.[5] It is a paradox that in German histories of the division of their own country, the insistence of each side on German unity continually increased. These demands for reunification and unity which were emphasized again and again on both sides of the Elbe, were the dissonant accompaniment to a process of division which allowed two German states to arise out of the German Reich, two states which, already today,

B

are arguing as to whether they can at all be considered as parts
of the same nation.

1. *Dokumente aus den Jahren 1945–1949. Um ein antifaschistisch-demokratisches Deutschland* (Berlin 1968).

2. Loewenthal, R., in *Europa und die Einheit Deutschlands,* Ed.
Hofer, W. (Cologne 1971), 307.

3. Doernberg, Stefan, *Kurze Geschichte der DDR* (3rd ed. Berlin
1968), 84.

4. ibid., 158.

5. ibid., 159.

2 | The interpretation of ideology and social reality in the GDR

I THE FUNCTION OF IDEOLOGY IN THE GDR SYSTEM

The standards, explanations and objectives of all political and social activity within the GDR system are provided by its ideology. It is the guideline for that socialist consciousness which the political leadership hopes to implant in all its citizens by a constant and steady stream of indoctrination. Since the founding of the state, its citizens have been subjected to a sustained effort by the political leadership to mould their attitudes and social behaviour to a socialist pattern. The incessant propagation of the prevailing ideology, the constant intrusion of politics at all levels, where political decisions are, at best, purely formal and never offer alternative ideas or standpoints for public discussion —all these are clearly an inevitable accompaniment to life in a socialist state. It is a political system which must constantly seek to affirm and justify from below the course decreed for it from above. In the GDR this constant stream of ideological propaganda stems from the wish to make people feel a socialist awareness. Whilst the party cannot depend on this new awareness, it will make use of such ideological propaganda in order to lead, and it will lose its totalitarian and repressive character in the same degree as the legitimacy of the system becomes ideologically more acceptable.

Thus the prevailing ideology also provides the intellectual structure intended to enable each citizen to comprehend his different social role correctly, and consciously to act according to his socialist understanding of it. Frequently this ever-present ideological framework is only loosely connected with mastering the concrete problems of everyday life, but it creates an atmosphere, a particular language, a scheme of personal orientation which penetrates into the life of every individual. For this reason it seems right to consider the basic features of the GDR's ideological consciousness more fully. This official consciousness is not identical with the actual feeling of the broad mass of the people about their society. Nevertheless, it permeates the whole structure of society and controls all its various aspects. In trying to understand the prevailing ideology, we shall get to know the political points of reference within the system and, at the same time, discover the aims and standards by which it hopes to be judged. Also we shall discover the general philosophy behind the way in which East Germans must come to terms with the actual awareness of their society.

2 POLITICAL AND IDEOLOGICAL SELF-AWARENESS

The official ideology of the GDR sees the foundation and development of its own state and society as being firmly rooted in the natural and lawful development of world history and ending with the triumph of socialism over capitalism and imperialism. It was only after the October Revolution (under the leadership of Lenin and based on the academic teachings of Marx and Engels) had made the first breach through the hitherto closed system of capitalist imperialism, that the era of transition from capitalism to socialism dawned on a world-wide scale.

According to current Communist doctrine this era of transition in world history is characterized by a fundamental conflict which affects the historical development: the conflict between socialism and capitalism. In the Marxist view, capitalistic states necessarily take on imperialistic characteristics in that they wish to bring non-capitalistic states under their own domination. The Federal Republic's policy of non-recognition and its isolation of the GDR on a world-wide scale during the fifties and sixties— until the Brandt/Scheel government brought about a more normal relationship between the two—encouraged the suspicion of expansionistic desires on the part of the Federal Republic. However, the participation of the GDR in the invasion of Czechoslovakia by the socialist states shows that even so-called socialist states do not shrink from imperialist actions. This conflict would seem to be gaining increasing significance in view of the successes and growing importance of the socialist countries in international politics; and be further strengthened by intensified conflicts within the capitalist system itself. Both factors inevitably give rise to the class struggles between imperialism and socialism which, according to communist ideology, must lead with historical inevitability, if perhaps not directly, to the final victory of the socialist system in the world.

The special significance of the GDR in this world-wide struggle lies in the fact that the era of socialism would now seem to have begun for Germany (if only, at first, for one part of the country) because of the establishment of a socialist state on German territory. As interpreted by the ideology of the GDR, the conflict between imperialism and socialism in the German region becomes particularly apparent in the marked contrast between the systems of the Federal Republic and the GDR. However, just as 'formerly medieval feudalism had to give way to capitalism, so today capitalist rule must give way to a socialist society throughout the whole world and thus also in Germany. The future belongs to socialism in the whole of Germany and not only in the GDR.'[1]

In this way the national class struggle between the two parts of Germany becomes part of an international conflict. From an East German ideological standpoint the GDR has already embarked on its future. It has entered 'the new, socialist era' in Germany. The goal of the revolutionary workers' movement in Germany has therefore already been achieved in the GDR in its practical realization of socialism and the true socialist community.[2]

Today the GDR sees itself as a developed socialist society well on its—perhaps not altogether clearly marked—way towards communism. The historical development of the GDR up to the present time has been sub-divided in official writings into three periods. The period from the end of the war to the founding of the republic (1945–9) is called the 'anti-Fascist democratic upheaval'. This is followed by the second phase of 12 years, the 'transition from capitalism to socialism' beginning with the creation of the GDR and ending with the building of the Berlin wall in August 1961. Not until reliable protection was thus afforded to its boundaries did the essential conditions exist for the comprehensive and systematic establishment of socialism in the GDR (third phase). This is the historical phase of development, which decisively affects the present. In this third phase it is intended that the vaguely stated pre-conditions for the transition from socialism to communism shall be created.

Even without following the linguistic definitions of communist ideology, one can see this division into three distinct periods of development as a meaningful method of writing the history of East Germany after 1945. The years up to the founding of the GDR form a closed period of history, as is also true of the western zones. Although for practical purposes the relationship between the Soviet occupying power and the occupied territory did not change markedly even after the formation of an East German state, the establishment of the GDR was nevertheless a formal step and an historic turning-point in the internal ordering of the state. When the GDR was founded in 1949, the socio-economic and political conditions necessary for the establishment of a socialist society had already been created as a result of the 'anti-Fascist democratic upheaval' brought about with massive Soviet support: these were the removal of power from the middle classes and the relatively unopposed leadership of the Communist Party. Building on these foundations, it was now a question of putting socialist principles into practice in all spheres of the economy and of society. Since these efforts were partly hampered by internal resistance, by rivalry with the adjoining western system and most of all by the tendency of innumerable citizens of the GDR to flee to West Germany, the almost unhindered enforcement and development of socialism in the GDR could only begin after the building of the wall in 1961. To this extent the building of the wall heralded a period of increasing consolidation in the GDR both internally and externally, manifesting itself in a growing self-awareness of the state and of society.

In the first phase, that period of 'anti-Fascist democratic upheaval' leading to the setting up of the socialist system, the establishment of socialism was not yet the declared aim of the Communist Party. Rather it was a question of establishing a 'parliamentary democratic republic with every democratic right for the people'. (KPD foundation proclamation). The political means used by the Communist Party to ensure its dominance were 'block politics', in other words, the amalgamation of all political parties including the more right-wing ones into an 'anti-Fascist democratic block'. In addition the domination of the Communists was assured by the more or less enforced amalgamation of communists and socialists into a Socialist Unity Party (SED).

This first period in the development of East Germany was also characterized by a process of decisive changes in the economic and social structure, by means of agrarian and industrial reforms. These, it is true, did not yet imply collective farming or complete state control of industry, although they did deprive the middle classes of the bases of their economic power. The integration of all political and social groups into a unified movement under the leadership of the SED was the internal political pre-condition for the next step, the transition from democratic to socialist revolution in the second phase. Thus the 'anti-Fascist democratic administration' became the 'state of workers and farmers', interpreted by party ideologists as a specific form of a proletarian dictatorship.

From an economic and political standpoint, the second phase of the history of the GDR was characterized by a rigorously planned economy on the Soviet model, in home affairs by the equally rigorous consolidation of SED leadership according to Stalinist principles. It is true that following the 20th party conference of the Soviet Communist Party, a number of difficulties in adapting to the new situation of de-Stalinization arose as did deeply-rooted differences of opinion as to a correct economic policy. However, the enforcement of collective farming in East Germany up to 1960 and the establishment of trade production co-operatives (supplemented by an ever stronger repression of the remaining private concerns) were further stages on the way towards socialism. The fact that at the beginning of this second phase the régime was by no means unshakable became explosively apparent on 15 June 1953 when an indignant protest by Berlin workers against the raising of their production quotas led to a downright revolt throughout the whole of the GDR which could only be put down with the help of Soviet tanks.

All in all, this second phase of transition to socialism is characterized by a mass of difficulties noticeable even in the internal power struggles within the leadership, in which Walter Ulbricht consistently held his own as leader of the SED. These difficulties were both economic and political in nature. Economically the

GDR lagged far behind its planned and stated aims and came to grief, especially as regards the standard of living, in attempting to demonstrate the superiority of the socialist over the capitalist system. This was made abundantly clear to the leadership of the GDR above all by the fact that hundreds of thousands of its citizens, mostly skilled workers, fled to the Federal Republic by way of West Berlin from economic as well as political motives. When in 1958 the allies steadfastly rejected Khrushchev's ultimatum demanding that West Berlin be given new status as a demilitarized 'free city', economic considerations eventually led to the building of the Berlin Wall in 1961, thereby completely cutting off the territories of the GDR from those of the West.

Politically too it had not been possible in this phase to achieve the desired solidarity between the East Germans and their state nor their loyalty to the government and its ruling party. It was only after the wall had completely sealed off the frontier with West Germany that the process of consolidation within the GDR could begin, leading—for better or worse—to a greater readiness on the part of the general population to identify with their state. Both from an objective historical standpoint and in the SED's own interpretation, 13 August is a turning point in the inner development of the GDR.

With the principle of collective farming enforced by the end of the 1950s and the 'reliable' safeguarding of the state frontier, the second period, the transition from capitalism to socialism came to an end and gave way to the third period, the extensive establishment of socialism which reaches into the present time. The previous period had seen the taking-over of state power by the socialist working classes and the creation of socialist industrial conditions, but had not yet achieved a universal realization of socialism: now, in the new phase, all efforts were to be concentrated on extending the principles of socialism into all spheres of society.

The GDR's division of its history into phases can be explained more clearly by seeing it simply as an evolutionary process of a new political system. The first phase was concerned with the creation of the fundamentals of the system by means of the so-called 'anti-Fascist democratic upheaval', the second with its enforcement by means of power politics and the third with the systematic and extensive application of its aims. The completion of the system within communism is planned for the distant future.

The key concept for the ideological interpretation of the political system of the GDR is the idea of socialism. 'What is socialism?' is the rhetorical question posed by the SED party programme, which goes on to give the following answers:

1. Socialism is the assumption of power by the most progressive social class, the industrial workers. They exercise the power of state in co-operation with agricultural and other workers in active employment in the interests and for the good of the people as a whole.

2. Socialism is the taking over of all wealth, all large-scale industrial production, all mineral resources and all land by the people. All work together and thereby continually create new wealth for all. Profits for the few and the exploitation of the many are abolished, the causes of economic crises and of unemployment are removed for ever.

3. Socialism is the attainment of a high rate of productivity, the application of the latest scientific knowledge and technology in the furtherance of a planned improvement of living conditions for the people; socialism is the realization of the basic principle: 'From each according to his ability, to each according to his achievement'.

4. Socialism is the realization of equal opportunities for all people. The achievements of culture, science and technology are to be equally available to all workers.

5. Socialism is a new quality in human relationships characterized by friendly co-operation and mutual help. It is the beginning of a society of free people inspired by the principles of a socialist morality. These are: socialist patriotism and internationalism, a feeling of responsibility towards the community, a love of work and strict working discipline.

6. Finally, socialism is a peaceful form of society, since in the GDR power is no longer in the hands of social classes which are interested in exploiting foreigners or oppressed groups amongst their own people. The form of socialism described above represents the first phase of communism, in which the age-old longing of mankind for freedom, equality and brotherhood, peace, humanity and justice will one day be finally fulfilled.

Socialism as a political system is identical in meaning with the term 'socialist democracy'. This concept, which plays an important part in the terminology of GDR ideology is explained tautologously as 'democracy of the socialist social and state order'.[3] What is meant here is the transposition of social and state domains within the framework of a developed socialist system. In a socialist democracy, it is said, equally tautologously, the dialectic between state and social development under socialist conditions becomes effective.[4]

Thus the concept 'democracy' is also reserved for the new phase of social development. Whilst the first period in the development of the GDR served to bring about the 'anti-Fascist democratic upheaval' that is, the complete setting up of a general democracy, and at the same time was a preparation for socialism, the new phase of an extensive establishment of socialism is considered as being democratic to an even higher degree. The term 'socialist democracy' is intended to express this higher stage of development. It implies that in the GDR the new structure of society created as a result of the triumph of socialist conditions in industry corresponds to the democratic institutions of the state. In the socialist state, so it is claimed, the polarity between state and society no longer exists in contrast to the capitalist state. In the socialist democracy, the dichotomy between citizen and private person, inherent in a capitalist state, is abolished; it is impossible to separate the socialist state—unlike the capitalist-liberal one—from the domains of society and the individual.[5] The political system is described as a 'total social system' extending into and including all regions of man's social life from the smallest community to the highest state authority.

In the official interpretation given by the GDR, socialist democracy thus has the task of preparing the ground for a change in social relationships in order to extend the range of socialism. It aims at co-ordination, at effecting agreement between divergent interests, at educating and disciplining all sections of society for the building up and protection of the socialist order. 'The socialist democracy is thus seen to be a unit composed of democratic institutions, social relationships and the conscious actions of its citizens, all of which are determined by aims based on the socialist interests of the whole.'[6]

3 THE EAST GERMAN CONSTITUTION OF 1968

The GDR's interpretation of its own ideology in the third phase of its development is expressed in the Second Constitution of the German Democratic Republic. It was drafted at the end of

1967, then publicly discussed and acclaimed and finally passed on 26 March 1968 by a referendum majority of 94·5%. The new constitution is intended to express the completed transformation of the GDR into a socialist state: indeed, the preamble specifically speaks of it as a socialist constitution. It replaced the first GDR constitution which came into force on 7 October 1949. This resembled a bourgeois democratic constitution in many essential respects and frequently corresponded both verbally and in substance to the constitution of the Weimar Republic. Admittedly the first constitution had hardly reflected actual political conditions; its content was interwoven with the systematic process of transforming the GDR into a socialist state. It was therefore no more than a natural consequence of the democratic upheaval toward socialism that the SED proposed a new constitution. This was to remove the disturbing discrepancy between a text which still showed a bourgeois interpretation of democracy and a political and social order resulting from a socialist upheaval.

Of course the new constitution is deliberately not seen as a new beginning, but as an expression of the continuous development of the GDR. The GDR constitution clearly sets out its ideological interpretation of a socialist democracy in a series of general and basic principles. These include the following:

1. Control of the state by the working classes and their Marxist-Leninist party. (Art.1).

2. The new formulation of the principle of sovereignty of the people: according to Article 2 of the constitution, all authority, without division of powers, is exercised by the workers with the aim of constantly seeking to perfect the socialist system.

3. The following are to be taken as fundamental to the socialist system:

    (a) the alliance of industrial and agricultural workers and all others in active employment.

    (b) socialist ownership of the means of production.

    (c) the planning and management of social development according to the most progressive scientific findings.

4. The most important structural principle of the constitution is democratic centralism, defined as 'the basic principle of state organisation'. (Art. 47)

5. The GDR pledges itself to support the 'principles of socialist internationalism' with special reference to co-operation and friendship with the Soviet Union. (Art. 6)

6. The granting of basic rights is bound to the general constitutional principles of the socialist democracy and at the same time linked to the safeguarding of corresponding duties.

One must regard the constitution of the GDR not so much as a juridical framework in the western sense, regulating the power of the state and its organs and ensuring a certain amount of individual freedom for its citizens, but rather as a firm belief in the socialist order, permeated with countless regulations for the organization of the state. The Constitution of the GDR is at the same time both a statute presenting a socialist organization and a socialist catechism.

4 ATTITUDES TO SOCIETY IN THE GDR

Because empirical enquiries and analyses are not possible, we do not possess a sure scientific way of discovering the actual attitude of citizens of the GDR to their society and their particular living conditions. Nevertheless there are some points of reference which enable us to obtain an appropriate picture of the actual political and social system of the GDR and how it has grown up under the influence and atmosphere of the official ideology. Hermann Rudolph has made the most impressive attempt so far to penetrate the true shape and inner interpretation of East German society, hidden behind the veil of ideology and the façade of state apparatus.[7] We are indebted to his book *Anmerkungen zum Leben im anderen Deutschland* for a number of the points made below.

The gulf between a comprehensive ideology with which the East Germans have to live day by day and their own personal experience of life is great indeed. Even so, the ideological stream into which everything that happens in the GDR has to be dipped is a very real element in the system. The social reality is formed by coming to terms with the ideological horizon set and delimited by the political régime. On the one hand this means that all social activity must somehow come within the ideological context and be interpreted according to the right formulae, on the other the obtrusive and ever present ideology leads to mistrust and indifference towards its current ideological content. It is not taken as seriously as it should be. One gives what is demanded, but does not really identify with what one gives. The ideology remains external and does not supply any effective conscious motivation for behaviour as it should do. Simply because the ideological momentum is so all-pervasive, the individual remains rather indifferent to it. It is just accepted, its formulae are recited if necessary, but as a rule it is not an integral part of the individual's life or what he makes of it. For this reason the socialist consciousness exists only in a very imperfect form in the minds of most citizens of the GDR and its political system.

Despite all this, the positive awareness of an identity with their state and social system possessing a character of its own and with some achievements to its credit, has grown strongly during the last few years, as many observers have noted. This awareness developed only in the 1960s. During the Stalinist era of the first ten years, the GDR leadership had imposed the new socialist forces on the people with a certain amount of repression and without much concern for the wishes or interests of the citizens. The opportunity for the creation of a specific awareness of the intrinsic merits of GDR society did not come until the majority of people realized that they could no longer pin their hopes on the Federal Republic and the western nations for a solution to their problems and that the Berlin Wall represented a final separation. This, together with the simultaneous relaxing of repressive rule on the part of the political leadership, gradually brought about a change in the fundamental attitude of most people. As a result of its achievements and successes, society in the GDR attained a sense of its own worth, which it had not succeeded in acquiring during the 1950s. It discovered, not without pride, that amongst the countries of the eastern bloc it was industrially the most progressive and with regard to the general standard of living, the most prosperous; it discovered, too, that the 'golden west' was never as golden as had generally been suggested; it suddenly developed a kind of national pride in its own achievements, for example in the fields of sport and education.

This undeniable sense of the intrinsic merit of GDR society naturally goes some way towards meeting the prevailing ideology, which had always expressed such ideas; however it does not arise directly out of this ideology but is a product of a positive coming to terms with the system. The models of socialist behaviour, as propagated by the political leadership, are only socially effective to the extent that they coincide with attitudes which do not belong solely to the socialist ideology, for instance a desire for order, for evaluating and recognizing achievements in work, for preserving the interests of the community in contrast to a pronounced individualism. For all these the ideology is only a kind of rhetorical accessory. This means, however, that the recognizable and relative success of the efforts of the political leaders to make the socialist system of the GDR acceptable and even justifiable to its citizens, depends strongly on the activation of traditional German values and attitudes and not primarily on the persuasive power of communist ideology as such.

As the internal development of the GDR makes clear, the acceptance of a political system by the citizens of a country depends essentially on whether this system appears to them lawful and just and whether it can guarantee the individual both personal security and a certain amount of prosperity. Since, however, the citizens of the GDR had from 1946 been forcibly driven towards a socialist society by permanent pressure from their leaders—which would have been impossible without massive and monopolistic coercion by the law and the apparatus of state—the political system only possessed a thin and very superficial basis of legitimacy during its first twelve years. As the expectations and hopes of a good standard of living improved, noticeably during the 1960s, so too did attitudes change. 'The less one has to stand in queues; the less the danger of being burdened with extensive laws; the more individual achievement is respected and rewarded and the more accurately it is possible to calculate one's expectation of moderate prosperity—all the greater becomes the tendency to concede legality to the GDR as a whole and thus also to its political system.'[8]

Nevertheless, the acceptance of the régime does not automatically extend to the ideological interpretation, disseminated by the ruling party, to which we have referred above. For instance it is highly questionable whether the industrial or agricultural worker in the GDR takes a special pride in living in a 'workers' state'; he considers it of far greater importance to receive a just wage, to find good working conditions, to be taken seriously and not least that in his free time he has both the means and the leisure to follow individual interests. Even from the political and ideological sphere, however, some fundamental ideas have penetrated into the actual self-awareness of East German society; today most of its citizens are convinced that their system ensures more social equality and justice than the capitalist democratic system of the West. Most of them believe that their educational system is socially more just and more efficient than that of the Federal Republic. Furthermore, the health services, guaranteed employment and social security in general are considered to be advantages of the system. Reports about abuses, glaring inequalities and injustices in a capitalist society cause a certain amount of satisfaction in the GDR since it is felt that they do not exist there. All this has led to a much more positive attitude towards the political system.

The tactical method of the régime to credit all its successes to party policies and the deeds of its socialistically-guided citizens boomerangs back in so far as blame for existing deficiencies in welfare, the building programme or industrial organization is automatically attributed to the political leadership. Anyone who claims, as do the political leaders, to have guided the state so far along its way, anyone who continually asserts the superiority of this state over the Federal Republic must also accept that responsibility for the failures, unpleasantnesses and deficiencies shall, like its successes, be laid firmly at the door of the political system.

Four factors have had a particular influence on the state of GDR society today:

1. The pressures and individual characteristics of a modern industrial society.
2. The constant process of moulding by the political system and its ideology.
3. The continuing effect of traditional German qualities as for instance a love of order and community traditions.
4. The actual historical experience of the gloomy post-war period, in which the occupying power and the German authorities forcibly clothed the old society in the new dress of socialism.

It is out of these elements that the reality of East German society has been formed; in coming to terms with them it has become what it is today. How then does the East German society of today see itself?

This society is a modern industrial society, its everyday life is determined by the principle of a constantly increasing industrial production and improving productivity. It is not by chance that the economic system is considered to be the cornerstone of the social system. At the centre of the social system is work, which is also the central category in Marxist anthropology. Whereas, however, the industrial societies of the western kind are more strongly consumer-orientated and generally measure their success by what they can produce for the true or the manipulated private interests of the individual, the industrial society of the East German kind is largely moulded by the demands of the political system. This is not concerned so much with the interests of the individual as producer and consumer, but rather with the collective interest, with the aim of making the private and social interest coincide completely. Because of this the free scope left to the East German citizen is altogether much more limited and more controlled than in the western industrial societies. The ever-recurring conflict between specialist and functionary is typical of the structural contrast between consumer-orientated and politically-orientated systems; the efforts of the East German leadership to blunt this conflict as far as possible by educating the indispensible specialist to adopt consciously socialist attitudes is very characteristic.

Certain typically German traits, stemming from the old national traditions cannot be overlooked in East German society today. 'East German society too must be understood in the light of a conglomeration of life-styles, behavioural patterns and value judgments by means of which the Germans throughout their history felt themselves to be German and which characterizes them in the eyes of their neighbours. . . . It values order, hard work and conscientiousness, it has a weakness for *Gemütlichkeit* . . . and it is prepared to adapt and to submit to discipline for the sake of some highly esteemed virtue'.[9] It is clear that these national characteristics which were modified much more strongly in the most recent developments in West Germany than in the East, are helpful to the political system. It is not by chance, as has frequently been pointed out, that the population of eastern Germany has always lived under some kind of authoritarian state or dictatorship during the last 100 years with the exception of the short and confused historical phase of a free way of life under the Weimar Republic.

Finally it must not be forgotten that the post-war period lasted much longer for the East Germans than for those in the West. Not only were conditions particularly hard under Russian rule and the Stalinist régime of the 1950s, but even within the eastern bloc the East Germans only had very limited freedom of movement. It is obvious that the East Germans must see the improvements in living conditions and mobility which have taken place, together with a lessening of political pressure, against the background of the sombre post-war years which they themselves experienced. One result of the post-war period is a certain still-effective immunity of the East Germans to the official ideology; on the other hand, they had to learn, during these years, to live with the new régime and come to terms with it.

The strengthened self-awareness and feeling of national individuality which the East Germans have attained since the 1960s and which is both cause and consequence of the inner consolidation of the East German state, is not an awareness of the state as the GDR ideologists would have it. It is, however, a politically most relevant phenomenon which, the longer it continues, removes the foundations from the West German idea of a single nation. The socialism of the GDR today is no longer simply a matter of political institutions and ideology as it seems to western observers, it has also, in a specifically German variant, penetrated into the social ideas and behavioural patterns of the East Germans themselves. Contemporary East German society lies in an intermediate zone between the old, from which it originates historically and the new, which the political leadership hopes to make of it.

1. SED manifesto of 1963.
2. ibid.
3. Haney, G., *Die Demokratie-Wahrheit, Illusion, Verfälschungen* (Berlin 1971), 160.
4. ibid.
5. ibid.
6. ibid., 196.
7. Rudolph, Hermann, *Die Gesellschaft der DDR—eine deutsche Möglichkeit?* (Munich 1972).
8. ibid., 104.
9. ibid., 40–1.

3 | The SED and the National Front

Strictly speaking the GDR is not a one-party state, but the four other parties which are linked to the SED through the block system and within the organizational framework of the National Front no longer possess any real independence. Block system means that the political parties of the GDR are grouped together as one active unit under the leadership of the SED, whilst, however, retaining their formal organizational independence. The block principle originated as a result of the conquest of Fascism after its military defeat during the Second World War. At that time one spoke of an 'anti-Fascist block'. The organizational aspect of this principle is seen in the alliance of the National Front. It affects the political programmes of all parties, the electoral system and, indeed, all parts of everyday political life. One therefore speaks of block politics, block elections, block committees, block parties etc. In practice the four parties and the *social* giant organizations no longer function independently of the SED. They have expressly acknowledged the leading role of the SED. The GDR is therefore a one-party state in fact, although it is content, for a variety of reasons, to accept the leading role of the Socialist Unity Party within the system and does not insist on the abolition of the other parties. When a political party is able to control the expression of political opinion in a state so extensively as does the SED, and when the 'alliance' between the ruling party and the others is such that the SED can always impose its own will against all opposition, the preservation of a multi-party system serves in the first place to integrate all sections into the political system dominated by the Unity Party without distributing power. It is then simply a question of political expediency whether the majority party wishes to become the sole party, as is the case in the Soviet Union, or whether it recognizes certain political advantages in continuing its alliance with the other permitted political groups. The SED has decided in favour of formally retaining a multi-party system. The National Front in which 'the parties and giant organizations all unite to act together to develop the socialist society' has been embodied in Article 3 of the new Constitution of 1968 as the 'alliance of all the people'.

The advantages which the ruling party in the GDR may see in retaining an alliance structure as opposed to pure one-party rule, have never been expressly stated. The following points may, however, have played a part:

1. The retention of a multi-party system preserves the semblance of a certain democratic pluralism and is easier to defend against the arguments of bourgeois democrats than a pure one-party state.

2. The parties and giant organizations outside the SED are better suited to bring about the necessary integration of all citizens into the GDR than the Communist Party itself, which meets with greater reservations amongst certain sections of the community than the originally bourgeois parties.

3. The existence of other parties allows the SED to shape its own role as the party of the working classes more clearly and to achieve greater ideological unanimity amongst its members. A comprehensive communist peoples' party might have to show greater flexibility than an élitist communist nucleus which can place greater emphasis on unanimity and discipline.

What is important in understanding this balance of power is the fact that all the political and social organizations which group themselves around this nucleus of the political system—the SED—within the National Front are unable to present a serious challenge to the dominating role of the Socialist Unity Party. All of them are simply auxiliary troops without independent command. Meanwhile the dominant role of the 'Marxist-Leninist party of the working classes' has been legally embodied in Article 1 of the Constitution. This clearly shows that in the GDR the Socialist Unity Party is intended to be the principal wielder of power for all time.

Without doubt the SED is the central political force in the GDR. It controls the party system, the apparatus of state and all social and cultural life. The GDR is the state of the Socialist Unity Party.

2 THE HISTORICAL DEVELOPMENT OF THE SED

The SED, originating from the enforced fusion of KPD and SPD, began as a typically left-wing party of the masses. On amalgamation it already possessed 1·3 million members. This number rose within two years to almost 2 millions, out of a population of then 19 millions. The ideological basis of the party in its beginning stages was the theory of a special German way to socialism. It aimed at an intermediate way between Communism and Social Democracy. From the outset, admittedly, tensions existed between the Social Democrats and the Communists inside the Unity Party, resulting in a gradual repression of the Social Democratic element in the party—some 'old Communists' were affected by this too—but in the main, the SED remained the left-wing party of the masses, possessing some democratic traits. Although the Communists clearly played the leading role, they by no means enjoyed unlimited dominance. Between 1946 and 1948 the SED was a socialist people's party.

This changed abruptly one year before the founding of the GDR. As a consequence not only of the resistance by Yugoslav Communists under the leadership of Tito against Soviet control, but also of the intensification of the cold war, the Soviet Union felt obliged to link all communist parties more closely to the Communist Party of the Soviet Union and to make all its organizational and ideological principles binding upon all the others. This resulted, from the year 1948, in the transformation of the SED into a Marxist-Leninist campaigning party, strongly committed to modelling itself on the Soviet prototype. In the eastern zone this transformation was brought about under the slogan of creating a 'new type of party'. Historically, however, the 'type of party' was not new. Rather it was a case of consistently applying the Soviet principles of party organization and management, as first propounded by Lenin and interpreted by Stalin, to the SED.

In the course of creating the new type of party, the SED was
purged of all 'hostile elements' and committed uncompromisingly
to the teachings of Marxism and Leninism, especially the Leninist
principle of 'democratic centralism'. From then on it called itself
a revolutionary campaigning party, the storm troops of the
working classes. The results of the transformation process were
'the enforced differentiation of the party into members and
functionaries of different ranks; the adoption of the organization
and principles of the Soviet Communist party; the anchoring
of the party in industrial concerns; the orientation against "Social
Democracy"; the recognition of the leading role of the Soviet
Union and its Communist Party; the demand for strict "class
awareness" within the party; the prominence of the SED as
guardian of the working classes and its consequent claim for
leadership as against all classes, sections and organizations.'[1]

In the West, this transformation of the SED after 1948 has
often been called the Stalinization of the party. Indeed, at that
time, the party completely committed itself to the Soviet party
model and the unconditional acceptance of Soviet control. Anton
Ackermann, a member of the Politbüro, who in 1946 had propounded the thesis of a special German way to socialism, had
to retract it two years later and then simply defined the new
type of party as being 'modelled on the party of Lenin and
Stalin'.

In order to 'purge' the party as considered necessary, a central
Party Control Commission was set up to investigate 'unreliable'
members and remove all opponents of the new theory, including
those whose social origins seemed to offer no guarantee for
maintaining a working class standpoint. These purges led to a
clear majority of party-line Communists over the Social Democrats at all levels in the party; however, they were not so comprehensive that the SED might consequently have lost its image
as the party of the masses. In the course of transforming the
party, the SED retained its relatively broad basis, yet the democratic character of party life receded ever more strongly into
the background, in favour of training reliable party nuclei.
Absolute power was ensured for the central party apparatus by
this new organizational structure. By means of its so-called 'cadre
politics' the party leadership systematically saw to it that only
those who were prepared to submit without argument to party

directives would be appointed to all important posts in party or state.

When, therefore, the GDR was founded in October 1949, the SED had already firmly established its political leadership within the system and was able systematically to strengthen it whilst building up the state. Within a short time, the SED had succeeded in making itself the leading all-controlling power in the new state and in removing or neutralizing all rival political groups.

All the same, the process of safeguarding and strengthening the power of the SED did not take place without some ups and downs and internal difficulties. The death of Stalin on 6 March 1953 provided the Stalin-orientated party with its first real test. Under its First Secretary Walter Ulbricht, the SED had faithfully responded to every step and change of direction in Stalin's policy and had eagerly supported the Stalin cult. The death of Stalin threw the party leadership temporarily off balance with regard to the new political and ideological developments. In addition, hopes rose amongst the East Germans after Stalin's death for a lessening of repression and for a greater degree of liberalism, hopes expressed also by some members of the Politbüro (Zaisser and Herrnstadt) who were pressing for the removal of Ulbricht and a change from the Stalinist party line inside the Central Committee. Because of the new balance of power in the Soviet Union and in the face of growing discontent amongst the people, the Politbüro did decide on a change in the party line, despite objections from Ulbricht at the beginning; it even admitted to a few mistakes, though in the end it was not Ulbricht himself but the members of the 'revisionist' group who were pressing for changes, who were removed from office. Ulbricht's claim to power during this phase was greatly aided by the revolt of 17 June 1953 against the dictatorial rule of the SED, which forced the new leadership in the Soviet Union to give Ulbricht their continued support.

In the following years, Ulbricht was able to strengthen his powerful position in the party still further. In contrast with developments in other Communist states such as Poland and Hungary, he even outlasted the most difficult period in the inner Communist policies of the post-war era, the phase of de-Stalinization, begun by Khrushchev at the 20th Communist Party Conference in 1956. Although the condemnation of Stalin by Khrushchev led to some compromises even amongst the leadership of the SED—Ulbricht himself was prepared to sacrifice Stalin's hitherto unshakable position as the classical upholder of Marxism to prevailing conditions—the party leadership cleverly avoided any intensive internal discussion on the criticism of Stalin and attempted to counteract internal difficulties by a policy of minor concessions to the people. However, following the events of autumn 1956 in Hungary and Poland, innumerable active groups formed within the SED which aimed at a decisive rejection of Stalinist principles. Criticisms levelled against these principles came in particular from the academic intelligentsia within the party. Its chief exponent was the philosophy lecturer Harich who, with his group, wished to adopt a 'third way' of socialist politics beyond capitalism and Stalinism. The aim of Harich and his colleagues was a 'human socialism' on the basis of certain democratic freedoms, as was pioneered in principle, though only briefly, by Dubček in Czechoslovakia twelve years later. Although in 1956 a dangerous falling apart of ideological unity and strength was apparent, Ulbricht succeeded in ridding himself of the opposing groups. Harich and his friends were taken to court and given prison sentences. At the highest party levels Ulbricht removed those colleagues who criticized his policies and pressed for the carrying out of internal reforms following de-Stalinization as well as for a less hostile attitude to the Federal Republic (Schirdewan, Oelssner and others). The tragic developments in Hungary in the autumn of 1956 contributed largely to Ulbricht's powerful position during this second and, for him, critical period.

Under the resourceful leadership of Walter Ulbricht the SED overcame all its internal difficulties; finally during the phase of inner consolidation of the GDR, beginning in the 1960s, its now firmly established rule was able to take on a less militant aspect. With the officially proclaimed ending of the transition stage from capitalism to socialism, the time had come at last for the party to give itself a programme, which it had not been prepared to formulate previously owing to the unclear political outlook. Admittedly the SED was encouraged in its efforts by the example of the Soviet Communist Party, which also drew up a new programme in 1961 and stood sponsor to the SED programme of

1963. In this the SED sees itself as the conscious and organized vanguard of the German working classes and all those in employment. Its firm ideological basis is Marxism and Leninism, the teachings of which it promises to apply creatively to actual prevailing conditions in Germany. It calls itself the Party of Peace and National Unity, the Party of Democracy, Freedom and Socialism. It assumes the leading role in all spheres of economic, political and cultural life of the republic, it seeks to develop a trustful, friendly relationship with all workers. It sees its main task today in encouraging its citizens to work towards the further growth of the socialist community. The SED is 'the highest form of organization of the working classes'.

Although the period immediately after the establishment of the GDR had been full of conflict, yet by means of concentrated learning and the friendly clarification of fundamental questions the party had succeeded in making Marxism and Leninism the basic principles of all their actions. Since then it had become increasingly obvious that 'the way prescribed for the working classes by the Marxist and Leninist party was both correct and successful'.[2]

After the inner consolidation of the régime by the building of the Berlin Wall, the SED could relax its grip and rule without the use of Stalinist methods. It even showed itself, especially in the economic field, to be capable of reform; thenceforth it laid particular emphasis on co-operation with science and endeavoured to carry out its leadership less by the rigid and dogmatic exercise of power but rather with the help of new administrative methods.

In this way the SED has increasingly succeeded in changing the style of rule it has exercised over East Germany since its independence from oppression of the people into some form of co-operation and consensus. The SED today is no longer a Stalinist party as in the 1950s, and the monolithic organization of the party appears looser in structure. It is no longer concerned so much with asserting its power by all means at its disposal including terrorism, but rather with the controlled consolidation of the leading role of a party which is now recognized as legitimate by an increasing number of GDR citizens as a result of a general improvement in living conditions.

3 THE ORGANIZATION OF THE SED

The basic principle of the inner party organization of the SED is Democratic Centralism. This formula, propounded and practised by Lenin, which has also become part of the new constitution of the GDR, is the fundamental principle underlying the whole of public and social life and in particular the internal party organization. Seen in general terms it implies election from below but control and direction from above. How these two elements are combined is seen especially within the party:

1. Members of all leading party organs must be elected democratically and are directly accountable to the organizations which elected them.
2. All decisions of the higher party organs are binding on the lower organizations within the party; they are to be carried out on a basis of strict party discipline; the minority must submit to the decisions of the majority.

Thus Democratic Centralism, as the term implies, contains both a democratic component, namely elections to the leading party organ, and a hierarchic component. Centralization ensures that the decisions of the highest authoritative body in the party shall apply to all subordinate organizations within it and must be carried out without argument.

In practice, the principle of hierarchic centralism certainly dominates at the expense of the democratic principle. The possibility of a democratic election of the authoritative bodies is limited in fact by the participation of higher party organs in drawing up most of the lists of candidates and in controlling the electoral process. Secretaries in the Central Office of the party who hold an important and powerful position in the SED at all levels are to be elected 'according to the instructions of the Central Committee' and are thus in fact given office from above. Thereby the democratic principle is strongly undermined.

Centralism thus ensures the observance and execution of all orders issued by the top party leadership. As a rule the party leadership (or more accurately the Central Committee, or its agent the Politbüro) lays down the fundamental political rulings, determines the institutional framework for executing its decisions and transfers responsibility for so doing to certain subordinate groups in the party. The mechanism of command which is called into play here may be either rigid or dictatorial, or may leave room for a 'creative' application of the fundamental political ruling. In contrast to the rigid chain of command during the Stalinist phase of the party, a greater flexibility of the party leadership has become apparent in the last few years, aiming, above all, to attain the co-operation of as many party members as possible.

An essential part of Democratic Centralism, on the other hand, is party discipline, which is expressly imposed upon members of the SED in their party statutes. Party discipline is intended to ensure unity and consistency in all party behaviour. As a party member, each individual is obliged to keep the interests of the party always before him and not only to respect the will of the party but also to fight for it, so that it is converted into action. What is demanded of each member is not only agreement with the basic principles and aims of the party, but also his active participation in building a socialist state. The statute book of the SED contains an extensive catalogue of obligations ranging from the duty to protect 'the unity and purity of the party' to the moralizing command 'to oppose over-optimism and any tendency to become intoxicated with success'.

The 'Basic Principles of Socialist Morality' laid down in 1958 have also become part of the catalogue of obligations. These require party members to show exemplary behaviour and constantly seek to improve all their faculties, especially their specialist and ideological knowledge. In general the hierarchic principle of centralism together with party discipline ensures the execution of the decrees laid down by the highest party authority. The most important and powerful body of the SED is the Politbüro, although it is only mentioned in passing in the statute book under the heading 'highest party authorities'. All that is actually said of it is that it will take over the political leadership of the Central Committee in between its plenary sessions. It is mentioned chiefly in connection with 'organizing the control of party decision and selection of party workers'.[3]

The SED Politbüro corresponds more or less to the executive of a large western party. As a rule it meets once a week and takes all decisions of political consequence. It is the permanent collective political leadership of the party and has the support of the secretariat of the Central Committee.

The Politbüro is elected by the Central Committee. Like all bodies of the SED it consists of full members and candidates, the number of candidates being about half the number of full members. Full members of management committees are recruited from these candidates. The actual size of the Politbüro is not specified by statute. It varies between 15 and 25 members including the candidates and thus corresponds roughly in size to the cabinet of a western government. The Politbüro is the leading political authority in the party and due to the close personal co-operation between members of the government and the Politbüro, its decisions apply with equal force to governmental policies.

Directly connected with the Politbüro as the collective management committee of the party is the Central Secretariat which is the administrative substructure of the party executive. It is manned by about ten full-time party secretaries under the departmental leadership of the First Secretary. The First Secretary—Walter Ulbricht until 1971, thereafter Erich Honecker—is the party chairman and the most important person in the political system of the GDR because of the dominant role of the party.

The Secretariat is the central party apparatus having over 1000 full-time staff. It is divided into several departments, each corresponding approximately to one of the main political spheres, with the addition of a number of purely party matters such as committee work and training. The party secretariat directs all the machinery of the SED from Berlin; its staff consists of about 50 000 paid full-time and about 300 000 honorary workers (out of a current total party membership of approximately 1·9 million).

It would seem from the party statutes which were revised for the fourth time in 1967 that the Party Conference is the highest authority in the party, followed by the Central Committee consisting of about 100 members and 50 candidates. (According to the statute, the Central Committee has to execute the decisions of the Party Conference and is considered as the chief authority between conferences.) However, both Party Conference and Central Committee are, in the first instance, concerned with legitimating and assenting to the decisions taken by the Politbüro and its administrative office, the Central Secretariat. Eight Party Conferences have so far taken place, the last in 1971. Party Conferences are now to take place only every five instead of every four years; the next Party Conference of the SED will thus be held in 1976.

Because of its size, the Central Committee is too unwieldy as an executive body. It meets about four times a year. It works through a number of standing and *ad hoc* committees of which the most important is the party Control Commission concerned with 'Unity and Purity'. Neither Party Conference nor Central Committees are debating bodies for working out guidelines of policy. They serve principally to confirm decisions taken by the leadership and to assent to them. The daily routine work of the party is carried out by the Secretariat. In so far as the questions are of general political significance the Politbüro always decides on measures to be taken.

The West has often called the organization of the top authorities of the Unity Party dictatorial. Indeed the principle of centralism does enable the leadership to exert a dominating influence on the party and on the formulation and execution of its policies. Nevertheless, the organization of the SED is not as different from that of democratic political parties as is always made out. Even in western parties the elected party leaders as a rule occupy a dominating position; even in western parties the Party Conference is frequently no more than a forum for confirming decisions taken by a party oligarchy elsewhere; even in western parties the party apparatus exercises an important function in regulating the life of the party. Yet a clear difference remains: in contrast to the western parties, the communist parties such as the SED have no really open discussion. Neither have its members the possibility of any effective influence in nominating candidates for party office. The extent to which the Unity Party has succeeded in its policies of centralization and discipline can be seen in the fact that all important resolutions are always passed unanimously.

The collective principle is binding on all leading party organizations, i.e. they are obliged 'to debate and decide all questions facing the party, as well as their tasks and the planning of work collectively'. (SED statute).

In this way at least a common process of discussion is prescribed for all administrative committees of the party and this prevents the taking of individual decisions by leading party members. In practice, the collective principle means that discussion takes place until a common line is gradually formed. Here of course the opinions of certain party members, especially the First Secretary, will carry much weight, but that is a natural process in all political decision-making.

The First Secretary, the Central Secretariat under him and the Politbüro led by him form the tip of the pyramid of power within the party. Its broad foundations are the so-called 'base organizations'. These are the smallest party units (corresponding to the former communist 'cells') of which there are over 500 000 in the GDR today. These 'base organizations' are considered to be the most important 'links between the party and the mass of the people' (Honecker). They carry out their work at grass-roots level, i.e. in industry, housing associations, administrative authorities, schools, etc. The aim is to put party decisions into practice in all spheres of life and to make citizens who are not party members aware of the constant presence of the party. Such base organizations are small controllable units which can be formed with as few as three members. They are grouped together by locality (*Ort*) and again by district (*Kreis*). The next level of the party structure is the area corresponding to the division of the country into 14 administrative areas called after their chief towns, plus the area East Berlin. The 15 area secretaries play a relatively important role within the framework of the party; each of them controls a secretariat of some size and as a rule these area secretaries are also members of the Central Committee. This completes the line joining the tip to the base of the party pyramid.

Because of the large membership which has shown no signs of decreasing, the party has laid much emphasis on the training and supervision of its so-called cadres, since its reorganization as a new type of party. The term 'cadre' signifies the leading groups of the party at all levels. Cadre politics are the politics of staffing. The party has worked out 'cadre principles' by means of which selection to the cadres is carried out. These include, amongst others, ideological reliability, strict adherence to party discipline, militant support of the party and a capacity for criticism and self-criticism. Smaller cadre groups work together in so-called 'party action groups' usually led by instructors from the central office.

As a result of the changing external and internal conditions under which the party has had to work since 1945, the party apparatus has frequently been reorganized in order to increase its effectiveness and power. During the last few years interest was centred in particular on its organization and structure to make the powerful position of the party more effective in all spheres of life on the one hand and, on the other, to avoid the ever-present threat of the party bureaucracy becoming too remote from membership and the general public. It is for this second reason that greater attention has recently been given to modern, scientifically based methods of leadership. Admittedly the party leaders have not given up the hierarchic principle of centralism, since this forms the basis of their undisputed rule, but they have taken care to see that individual party members now have a greater share of responsibility and can work with greater effectiveness.

For these reasons the SED no longer appears as a party led from above with dictatorial commands; it now gives scope to individual responsibility amongst its lower organizations, whilst retaining the unconditional claim to leadership for the highest party authorities. The increasing interweaving of everyday party work with the complex questions which arise in dealing with given economic and social tasks has contributed to a certain ideological relaxation of the party style and placed greater emphasis on a more rational, factual discussion even within the party. This tendency, which has been described by western observers as consultative authoritarianism is, incidentally, also expressed in the social composition of the party.

4 THE SOCIAL STRUCTURE OF THE SED

The SED calls itself the party of the working classes and all working people, but it is no longer a workers' party in the strict sense of the word. Admittedly it has always tried to recruit its members in the first place from amongst industrial and agricultural workers, but in the last few years men and women have increasingly taken up leading positions in the party who are not actually 'workers' but who have qualified in the universities and technical colleges of the GDR. According to statistics produced at the 7th Party Conference in 1967, 45% of the members are industrial workers, 6·4% agricultural workers, 28% employees, and of these 12% are academics. From these statistics the conclusion could be drawn that, compared with the social structure of the population as a whole, the industrial workers are under- and the academics over-represented in the SED. However, there is little sense in arguing that the SED is no longer a workers' party and not entitled to its ideological claims. The change of emphasis in the social composition of the party membership is a very normal process. To the extent to which the party had to deal with administrative tasks and controls throughout public life, it needed qualified experts and intellectuals. Almost a fifth of the present members and candidates of the party have graduated from a university. This shows both the general spread of higher educational standards in the GDR and the greater participation of academic experts in party work. The change in social structure in favour of those with academic training is seen most clearly at middle levels; almost all the secretaries of the district administrations of the SED today have received a university education.

Several sociological theories about processes of social change in the GDR leadership were inspired especially by the empirically thorough, subtle and consequently much praised investigation by P. C. Ludz.[4] Despite these theories, no convincing documented proof can, in our opinion, be established from the changes in the qualifications of committee members in favour of fiercer rivalry between the political nucleus of the party (which Ludz calls the 'strategic clique') and the more specialist party *élite* ('the institutionalized opposition *élite*'). Rather a reciprocal process of assimilation appears to have taken place amongst the leadership of the GDR which, on the one hand has enabled the old, still strongly ideological group to recognize the necessity of specialist, rational consultation just as, on the other, the specialists themselves were ready to subordinate their own specialisms to the greater ideological context and to appreciate the importance of close co-operation between academic study, practice and ideology. The much discussed conflict between dogmatists and pragmatists in the Central Committee which may perhaps have broken out here and there was certainly much less striking than was generally assumed. Today it is a fact that those academics who have recieved their training in the GDR do not question the political aims of the party leadership, so long as they are guaranteed a certain amount of freedom in their specialist field.

During the 1960s and in the course of consolidating the position of the GDR, the SED has become a more open, less dogmatic and politically more flexible party. The traditional revolutionary momentum of the class struggle has disappeared, to the regret of many of the original functionaries, but the party is now so firmly rooted in the total life of the republic, and especially in the apparatus of state, that the greater inner mobility and openness of the party can no longer shake its powerful position. On the contrary, it is now easier for the party than before to be accepted by the people and thus to extend the consensus of opinion in its favour which it sought to establish in vain during the 1950s.

5 PARTY AND STATE

The organizations of party and state are not identical in the GDR, but in accordance with its leading role in the state, the party does, of course, permeate the whole of the apparatus of state. In the first instance this happens by means of the same staff being in the principal bodies of both party and state. Leading party functionaries at the same time hold important offices of state, such as the Minister President Stoph who is also a member of the Politbüro of the SED. The majority of members of the Council of Ministers are also members or candidates of the Central Committee of the SED. The interweaving of state and party by means of common staffing is a perfectly normal process which is also characteristic of multi-party states of a democratic western type. There likewise the leading representatives of the ruling parties are also found in the most important positions of government. The difference consists in the fact that in the GDR the decisions of the party committees essentially determine the work of the state organs or at least their direction, whereas, if anything, the reverse is true in the western parliamentary states in that the governmental committees, such as parliamentary groups, largely determine the policies of the party.

This quite normal phenomenon of an interweaving of party and state through staffing is accompanied in the GDR by a more far-reaching coupling of these entities. This becomes effective at all levels of governmental activity, from the municipal to the national, by means of party members and party organizations within the apparatus of state. Party members who work in state administration are employed as such and not as independent functionaries. They are obliged, above all, to follow the instructions of their party. Thus the SED can influence state activities directly through its party members and organizations. The same is true of the giant organizations, as for instance the trade unions.

In practice, party and state in the GDR have become a good and effective partnership. They are only little affected by questions of legal authority. The distribution of work in the party apparatus (for instance in the specialist departments of the Central Committee) corresponds on the whole to its distribution in the state administration. Since the distinction between state and society in the GDR hardly possesses any significance in constitutional law, the co-operation between the state and the leading state party poses no great difficulties. Because of its improved standing in the total political system, the party has, in recent years, been increasingly able to lessen its direct interference in state administration by its party functionaries, as was still quite usual during the 1950s. Indeed, during recent years, the SED has promised officially to take less part in government and administration and simply to concentrate on 'key questions on social development'. This could only be done once the party was certain that the apparatus of state was working fully in accordance with the intentions and aims of the SED. Because of its organizations and methods of ruling the SED can, at any time, influence the state in any way desired, should conflicts occur. The fact that it need no longer make great use of this power simply shows to what extent party and state have fused together in the GDR and how much the GDR is the state of the SED.

6 THE REMAINING PARTIES OF THE NATIONAL FRONT

The National Front, originating from the People's Congress Movement for the Unity of Germany, officially founded on 7 October 1949, the day of the establishment of the state, is an

C

amalgamation of all the political parties and giant organizations of the GDR. In this, the SED, even if it does not have an absolute majority, plays the leading role. The new Constitution of the GDR calls the National Front the organized expression of the alliance of all the people. Its aim is said to be the union of all the people to work together for the development of the socialist society.

It is thus clearly stated that the National Front both as a whole and in its structurally independent parts has the same intentions and aims as the SED. One could also call the National Front the alliance of ruling parties and social groups in the GDR, the direction and aims of the state being determined by the party of the working classes, the SED. For this reason, political parties other than the SED have only a subsidiary, not a really independent function. The formal independence of the parties and giant organizations which is repeatedly emphasized by no means contradicts this. Since the beginning of the 1950s the four smaller parties and the giant organizations have been committed in their programmes to recognize the political leadership of the SED and to support the formation of a truly socialist society.

The block of anti-Fascist democratic parties going back as far as 1945, out of which grew the National Front, can therefore only be called a 'multi-party' system in a formal sense. Because the proportional strength of the parties and giant organizations in the representative bodies of the republic, notably the People's Chamber, is unalterable, it can have no inner political dynamism. In the People's Chamber, the SED has a constant number of 110 seats, the remaining four parties 45 seats each (not counting the members from Berlin), whilst the giant organizations are allotted a variable number of seats. At the head of these is the Alliance of Trade Unions with 60 seats. Only on a local level are slight variations in proportional strength permitted.

The National Front achieves this virtually constant proportion in the distribution of seats to the represented body by drawing up a single list of candidates and submitting it to the electorate for approval. On the strength of this list, which has to be accepted *en bloc*, the election result is predetermined from the outset, even before the actual election. It simply varies in the number of votes cast and even this only to a minimal extent, the question being whether the percentage of voters is nearer 99 or 100%.

Parties which can exercise no political dynamism by a direct appeal to the electorate are like mummified entities. The fact that they are nevertheless kept alive in the interests of the SED suggests that they have a certain necessary function within the political system.

Both Soviet and German communists, correctly assessing anti-communist attitudes amongst large sections of the German people, thought it preferable after 1945 to organize the middle-class sections of the community into political organizations of their own and to leave them a certain amount of independent scope. Thereby, and by giving them a share of political responsibility, they hoped to bring them into the new communist order and to bind them to it. The block of anti-Fascist democratic parties was intended to broaden the basis of political responsibility as much as possible and to relieve the SED of carrying this burden alone. The SED was always strong enough to make the fundamental decisions considered necessary, but these decisions were to be the joint responsibility of the bourgeois parties also. This was the whole point of block politics.

After the formal end of de-Nazification the Russians even went so far as to support the formation of two new 'bourgeois' parties, the National Democratic Party (NDPD) and the Democratic Agricultural Workers' Party, *Demokratische Bauernpartei* (DBD), in order to link those groups outside the régime more closely to it and to lessen the weight of the already existing middle-class parties (LDPD and CDU). The National Democratic Party was even allowed by the occupying power and the SED to make a limited amount of anti-communist propaganda. It was intended to act as a political focal organization for former National Socialists and National Conservatives. Indeed, the party saw itself in line with the 'national bolshevist' tradition of the 'League of Officers of the National Committee of Free Germany' founded after the German defeat at Stalingrad by communist emigrants in the Soviet Union. Allowing the formation of this party therefore served in the first place to integrate people with national interests into the socialist system. Furthermore at the time of the founding of the state, this party had the special task of emphasizing national tradition and the 'concern' of the GDR with all Germany.

In spite of the firm incorporation of the middle-class parties into the block ruled by the SED, opportunites still exist on the party level for points of contact with representatives from the corresponding parties in the Federal Republic. Their top leadership, political style and social composition all give the bourgeois parties a different party image from that of the SED. Now, as previously, certain bourgeois traits characterize these parties even though they have today become quasi-socialist parties and are hardly able to exercise any significant influence on politics as a whole.

In the beginning phase of block politics, on the other hand, (between 1946 and 1948) the political independence of these middle-class parties was stronger. The first tolerably free elections in the Soviet zone gave the Liberal Democratic party and the CDU each on average 20–30% of the votes in the five *Länder* of the east zone which existed at that time. The two parties were of almost equal strength and could after all count on the support of half the electorate. This is reflected in the composition of the first People's Chamber after the founding of the GDR. As a result of the single list prepared by the democratic block, which already included the giant organizations in addition to the political parties, the SED obtained 90 seats, the Liberal Democrats and the CDU 45 each, and the two new parties, the National Democrats and the Democratic Agricultural Workers' Party 15 each. Since the National Front was not formally constituted as the organized alliance of all the people until the establishment of the state, elections to the People's Chamber were dispensed with in 1949 and held instead in 1950. For the single list of candidates to be elected, a new system was brought in which gave the SED 25% of the seats, the Liberal Democrats and CDU 15% each and the two new parties 7·5% each, whilst 30% of the seats were reserved for representatives from the giant organizations. The most important amendment later made to this distribution was that the number of seats allotted to the two new parties was allowed to rise to that of the other bourgeois parties. This showed not only equal treatment of the non-communist parties, but also an attempt to bring them into line, since they now all had an equal number of seats in the People's Chamber.

In contrast to the leadership of the post-war years, the present chairmen of the four bourgeois parties are reliable administrators of the interests of the SED régime, without in fact being functionaries of the communist type. Under the prevailing conditions, the continued existence of bourgeois parties lessens the otherwise inevitable ubiquity of the SED. The SED is indisputably the decisive force in the National Front—which has for years spoken of itself as the mouthpiece of a broad socialist people's movement —but for everyday politics in the GDR and for those citizens spurred to political activity by the régime, it does make a difference whether other parties exist and whether citizens of the GDR can express their political views within the social framework of a party corresponding to their bourgeois origins or solely within the forms and concepts of communist party politics. To this extent the preservation of a multi-party system does, in spite of everything, signify some relativity in the system of one-party rule, which for many citizens undoubtedly appears as an advantage compared with a purely one-party system.

The erstwhile bourgeois parties also have industrial and agricultural workers amongst their members, but of course the main proportion of their membership comes from the former middle classes. Exact figures for current membership are not available. They are estimated for the CDU at far above 100 000, for the Liberal and National Democrats at about 100 000 and for the Agricultural Workers' Party (by no means confined only to these) far below that number. In any case, in the political situation in which these political parties have to act, membership figures are of no great significance. It is much more important that those citizens of the GDR who feel the need to play an active part in politics can do so within the framework of the former bourgeois parties if they have an insuperable prejudice against the SED. Thus, for Christians in the GDR the CDU is doubtless that political organization which can best take care of their political problems, even though it is hardly in the position to solve them according to the principles of the Christian churches. To a limited extent the subsidiary parties also exercise a certain protective function for certain groups amongst the population. The price which they have to pay for this marginal, but in individual cases not unimportant, role is their unequivocal acceptance of the socialist society and the political supremacy of the SED. At the beginning of the 1950s, the chairmen of the Liberal Democratic Party and the CDU had already declared their loyal support for the establishment of socialism. They expressly recognized the correctness of the fundamental economic analyses of Marxism and Leninism and beyond this attempted to embody their traditional ideals of Christian humanity and the free development of the personality within the social system directed by the communists of the SED.

The alliance of the National Front has proved to be a useful instrument in bringing about communist rule in an originally strongly anti-communist country, both in the early history of the GDR and in the later period of developed socialism. It serves to integrate all groups of people into the socialist order and even today still has a social and a political function. If this were not so, a purely one-party state would surely have taken its place in the new constitution of the GDR.

1. Förtsch, E., *Die SED* (Stuttgart 1969), 27.
2. Erich Honecker.
3. SED Statute Book, Article 41.
4. Ludz, P. C., *Partei-Elite im Wandel* (The changing party *élite*) (Cologne/Opladen 1968).

4 | The structure of the state

1 THE STATE AS AN INSTRUMENT OF SED
POLICIES

The attitude of western democrats to the state differs from that of communists in having a different conception of the relationship between the state and the social system. Whereas—according to western democratic theory—the unity of state decisions arises from a variety of opinions in a pluralist society, the socialist society is itself determined by the principle of unity because of the dominating rule of the Communist Party. Whereas, too, in the pluralist society of the liberal democratic state the expression of public will only becomes monistic as an end effect, the communist democratic state has a monistically structured society from the outset. From this it follows that the relationship of state and society must be different in each case. In the western system the function of the state is to integrate; it must convert a varied, heterogeneous social will into a uniform state will which society will obey. In a socialist society, on the other hand, competition between social groups and their varied interests does not arise because of the dominance of an all-pervasive political party and the absence of class conflict; therefore the state does not need to attempt to unify a heterogeneous social will. Nor does it need any special state mechanism to bring about integration, since the principle of unity is already present and does not have to be produced more or less imperfectly by majority rule, temporary rule or the art of compromise.

Out of this theoretical relationship spring some clear consequences for the role and function of 'state management' (as the new GDR constitution calls it) in the political system of the GDR. Socialist society functions through the state. Its uniformity is brought about by the control exercised by the working classes and this in turn by the leadership of the SED in the social process. The individual organs of state are simply the necessary organizations for safeguarding the social power of the working classes and their party and to carry out their political aims. The new constitution of the GDR advisedly speaks of the socialist society and 'its' state (Art. 2 para. 1). Since the question of power in society has already been resolved, the state in a socialist society can never assume any independence or act autonomously in society as is true of western democratic states (though from a communist standpoint they simply appear as instruments of one social class, namely the bourgeoisie). It therefore becomes apparent that the state and its organs are not the central political organization of the GDR régime. It is the party which plays the central part in politics. Through the Politbüro, the Central Secretariat and the First Secretary, the party and not the apparatus of state is responsible for all important political decisions affecting the life of the state. The party sets the political guidelines and impulses; it directs and controls the formation of political will and political decision-making, the effects of which are binding upon all organs of state.

In spite of the fact that the political will of the party and that of the state are identical in practice, the institutions of party and state are not, as a rule, the same in communist régimes. A state of affairs could well be imagined in which the Politbüro were identical with the government, the First Secretary of the SED were also the Head of State, and the Central Committee could act as the People's Chamber. There are however good reasons for the fact that in all totalitarian states, whether Fascist or communist, the fusion of party and state is not absolute, in other words does not lead to their institutions being identical with each other. The main reason is that the formal separation of the institutions of party and state provides the necessary precondition for the possible activation of the system by the ruling party at any time. A structure in which the institutions of party and state were entirely fused would, in the end, be a state without dynamism, without the stimulus and productive energy of a political movement. It would be a relatively rigid structure tending to orientate itself primarily by the private interests of those currently in power, as is the case with authoritarian régimes, and military dictatorships.

There is therefore a good deal to be said for keeping party authorities and state organs separate in the GDR. True, the fusion of key posts in party and state by means of staffing as well as the priority given to party directives by all party members working in state bodies essentially guarantees that the will of the party is carried out by the state and its organs. But just because the party stands outside the state it is able to make the state its tool for carrying out its will; just because it is the chief force in society it can continually influence the development of that society, far more than the state. In the case of the GDR it must be added that as a result of its historical development, the SED does allow the existence of other political and social groups, so long as these do not question its claim to leadership. For this reason too the fusion of state and party organizations would seem impossible.

Neither the GDR nor the Soviet Union are at present concerned with the question whether such a fusion of state and society could lead in the end to a virtual disappearance of the state function as such—a vision proclaimed in Marxist theory as the final end of history. The rule of the SED is, of course, bound to the exercise of power by the apparatus of state. This alone and the 'monopoly of physical force' (Max Weber) claimed by it can, in the last analysis, guarantee the continuance of that rule. A rejection of the apparatus of state by the SED would be tantamount to an abdication from its ruling position.

If the state is thus in the first place the instrument of power of the ruling Socialist Unity Party, then it must clearly be so organized that this function can become as effective as possible. One essential requirement for this is the principle of *unity of powers*. This basic principle had already been incorporated in the first Constitution of 1949 despite numerous relics of the liberal western system of shared powers. It is rooted in the new Constitution both in the formula of Democratic Centralism, as in the 'basic principle of the structure of state', and in the 'principle of the unity of decision-making and execution' (Art. 47, 48).

All this means that the various state bodies are not organized in a system of reciprocally limiting jurisdictions as is true (even if only in principle) of western democracies (cf. de Montesquieu's famous saying '. . . que le pouvoir arrête le pouvoir'). Rather they operate as one unit where the different state bodies simply exercise different functions. For the rest, the union of powers is only the necessary constitutional consequence of the premise that society in the GDR is determined by the rule of one social class in whose interests the state has to work. Social unity leads to unity of executive power, even if social unity is not fully realized, that is, if remnants of other social classes still exist. In such cases especially, the apparatus of state serves to hasten the process of unification by continuing the class struggle against these remnants. For this reason the dominance of the party over the apparatus of state is occasionally called the 'dictatorship of the proletariat', although this traditional Marxist formula is only seldom used in the GDR today on account of its militant character.

What is remarkable about the structure of the state in the GDR is that there no longer exists any government in the classical meaning of that word. There are two leading organs of government: the Council of State and the Council of Ministers. Both derive their authority from parliament. According to the Constitution, the Council of State unmistakably has the greater powers. Whereas the Council of Ministers has principally to administer the decisions taken by the People's Chamber and the Council of State, the latter is the competent authority in the legislative process, the final executive authority and, at the same time, the final authority in the legal system, since it interprets the Constitution and its laws and supervises the activities of the Supreme Court. The Council of State is the culmination of the constitutional principle of the unity of powers.

Since the election of Erich Honecker as party chief of the SED in 1971, he has been the most powerful man in the GDR, even though his predecessor, Walter Ulbricht, remained as chairman of the Council of State. This has led to a certain shift in the political weight of the various state bodies. Whilst under Ulbricht the most powerful state body was the Council of State, this now has less political importance under Honecker, whereas the Council of Ministers has increased in political stature. In this respect the 'Constitution of the Council of State' made to measure, as it were, for Ulbricht in 1968, already today no longer reflects the actual constitutional position of the GDR. This shows once again that in communist states it is the positions of power within the party which are the decisive factors in the relative importance of the state bodies and not the Constitution.

2 THE PEOPLE'S CHAMBER

It is true that the new Constitution of the GDR has devoted
a lengthy section with many paragraphs (Art. 48–65) to the
People's Chamber. Nevertheless, the political significance of
the 'supreme state authority' is negligible. This can be seen in
the fact that the Chamber meets surprisingly seldom. The People's
Chamber elected in July 1967 met 5 times in the second half of
1967, 7 times in 1968, only 3 times in 1969 and 4 times in 1970,
the meetings in each case lasting usually one day only. If the 13
to 15 committees of the People's Chamber did not have at least
some importance—not so much in their discussion of draft laws
as in having control over their execution—one would have to
regard the People's Chamber as a relatively unemployed organ
of state.

Formally the People's Chamber is there to create further
organs for the other central state bodies. It elects the Council
of State, the Council of Ministers, the National Defence Council,
the members of the Supreme Court and the Prosecutor General
yet in all these cases it simply ratifies decisions already made by
the central management committees of the ruling party. The
People's Chamber would exercise actual power if it could decide
on alternatives or were in a position to alter the proposals which
it is meant to confirm. In practice, however, this is not the case.
With very few exceptions, the People's Chamber reaches all its
decisions unanimously. The most notable exception of recent
times was the vote on a law on abortion which a few members
of the CDU were allowed to vote against. A parliament which
reaches unanimous decisions in principle is not an organ of
power but simply one of assent.

The number of laws passed is also small being, on average,
about 12 per year. This indicates that the People's Chamber
only deals with the more fundamental questions which help to
mould state and society, having assigned its authority with regard
to law-making largely to the other chief state bodies, especially
the Council of State and the Council of Ministers. Admittedly,
the right to initiate laws (introducing them in the People's Chamber) belongs not only to those representing the parties and giant
organizations in the People's Chamber, but also to their com-

mittees and even to the Free German Trades Union (thus increasing its importance amongst the giant organizations); however as a rule all draft bills are introduced by the Council of State or the Council of Ministers. In any case the Council of State plays the primary role in the process of law-making since it has the right to deal with all draft bills in advance and to examine them to see whether they conform with the Constitution. Thus it is the Council of State and not the People's Chamber which is the final authority on legislation. In addition, all laws, particularly those of general importance, must be drafted in accordance with the guidelines and suggestions of the ruling party, so that the People's Chamber in essence only has a formal part to play in this process. Only about half the laws are actually discussed in plenary session, whilst the unanimous acceptance of a law by all parties in the People's Chamber is the general rule.

The People's Chamber has 500 members, of whom 66 are from the Greater Berlin district. These, just like the Berlin representatives in the Federal German Bundestag, are not elected at the general elections (on account of the four-power status of the city) but are sent as delegates by the people of East Berlin. The members are subdivided into parties according to the organization to which they belong within the framework of the National Front, yet this is only of importance in the appointment of members to the various organs in the People's Chamber, which usually sees to it that such appointments are made from representatives of the different political groups and mass organizations. The parties and groups do not possess any political independence such that they could pursue individual policies. The strongest group (including the Berlin delegates) is the SED with 127 members, followed by the Free German Trades Union with 68, then the four block parties with 52 each, Free German Youth with 40, the Democratic League of Women with 35 and the League of Culture with 22. Most of the delegates of the giant organizations can in practice be grouped with the SED but even the four block parties have so small a political weight that without exaggerating the facts, one can regard the People's Chamber as the delegation of the SED.

The People's Chamber holds office for four years at a time. The members are elected in 'free, general, equal and secret elections' in accordance with the Constitution (Art. 54). The members of the People's Chamber are bound to keep in close contact with their electors. They must render account of their activities and 'attend to their electors' suggestions, ideas and criticisms'; they are obliged to keep times available for consultation and discussions with and on behalf of their electors. In this way a direct relationship of the People's Chamber to society is to be established. The formal dependence of a member on his electors goes so far that he can be removed by them if he 'grossly fails' in his duties.

From these conditions it has been deduced that the parliamentary representatives in the GDR are subject to an 'imperative mandate' from the electors. However, it is unthinkable that a member would heed any instructions from them that were not in line with the policies of the SED so that in fact these conditions must be seen as paying lip-service to the idea of a people's democracy whilst emphasizing the elements of Soviet democracy. In practice it is impossible for the electors to exercise any influence from below which might run counter to the principle of democratic centralism, safeguarded from above both in fact and by law. Nevertheless, the conditions mentioned above serve to ensure a certain relationship between the members and the mass of the people and to counteract the danger of estrangement between electors and elected.

Thus the People's Chamber, in spite of the various further functions given to it, is really a relatively unimportant political body. Its title of 'supreme state organ of power' may well be justified within the framework of the socialist conception of democracy because the People's Chamber represents the organized expression of 'the political power of the workers' in the state; yet the true wielders of power in the state—supported by the power of the leading political party—are the Council of Ministers and the Council of State. These are the central organs of political decision-making within the state.

3 THE FUNCTION OF ELECTIONS

Elections to the People's Chamber and other representative bodies cannot really be compared to elections in the western sense, in which the electors have the freedom to choose between personal and, in part, objective and ideological alternatives. The possibility of actual choice between persons and parties does not arise, since from the earliest beginnings of the GDR the people have always been presented only with the single list drawn up by the National Front. This single list (which gives the political parties and giant organizations with the number of seats allotted to them) is already identical with the outcome of the election. East German interpreters of politics nevertheless speak of free elections in the sense that there is no exploitation in the GDR—as is alleged of capitalist countries—but rather that the citizens themselves have become 'free' through their own productive work for a socialist society. The basis of freedom, therefore, is insight into what is socially necessary. Apart from this, so it is said, every citizen of the GDR can choose freely at elections.

It has also frequently been doubted whether elections in the GDR are really secret. The requirement that elections must be secret is formally fulfilled by having facilities (e.g. separate booths) at the polling stations so that votes can be cast in secret. This right is undermined by the practice of open voting, encouraged by the parties and giant organizations. Nobody, so goes the argument, should deprive a citizen of the right to voice openly his approval of the National Front candidates and of the policies of party and government.

In practice this means of course that social pressures are brought to bear on those who, in other circumstances, would make use of their right to vote secretly. Even so, ensuring that a secret ballot did take place would make no difference to the prefabricated outcome of the election; at most the number of invalid votes might increase.

The function of elections in the socialist system is misunderstood if they are regarded in the traditional way as being a method for approving *or rejecting* a policy and those who represent it. In socialist countries the only function of an election is to approve the prevailing system. Because this system sees itself by definition as progressive, as serving the good of the people and as ensuring 'a peaceful life', 'the planned increase in living standards' and 'the free development of the individual' (cp. Art. 4 of the GDR Constitution)—for all these reasons there cannot, according to official doctrine, be any opposition, since this would imply support for war, for bad living conditions and for non-freedom.

Accordingly, it would be impossible to offer different political alternatives, not even alternatives for different ways to socialism.

Thus elections have purely the function of general assent. At the same time they serve to mobilize and educate the mass of the people politically. The large-scale preparations for the elections—it would be wrong to call them an electoral battle—are intended to bind the citizens more closely to the system and to ensure their active support for those aims which the leading party prescribes for state and society. The actual ballot thus attains the character of a demonstration, it is 'an act of self-assertion by the socialist state'.[1] Election day is therefore not a day of political decision, when the sovereignty of the people becomes manifest, as in pluralist democracies, it is a day when the political system asserts itself and, in the eyes of the SED, even a red-letter day. For this reason too it is the ambition of the political leadership to get everyone who is entitled to vote to the polls if possible. Although there is no legal compulsion to vote, the percentage of voters is always close to 100%: in 1963 it was 99·25%, in 1967 98·82%. The higher the percentage vote that can be recorded, the higher is the rate of success, whereas seen from a western standpoint it is just this almost complete voting percentage which is regarded as an expression of coercive mobilization, making a farce of the whole election.

Nevertheless, in the preparatory stage of the election opportunities for choice (if not by the electors themselves) do occur to a limited extent: this is because the candidates, who are finally named on the single list issued by the National Front have first to be selected, initially by their own organizations and lastly by the National Front itself. By means of this procedure for the selection of candidates, the SED, as leading party within the National Front, has the opportunity not to include in the single list the names of those candidates of other parties or the giant organizations of which it does not approve. Even after the first compilation of the list it is able to make substitutions which it considers necessary. All candidates must introduce themselves to the electors at 'electoral conferences'. At such conferences it may happen that the selection committee of the National Front is told by the electors' organization that certain candidates ought not to be selected. In this way it is possible to test 'bourgeois' candidates in the first instance and then replace them by 'more suitable' ones if necessary.

By means of the single list and the additional control by 'electors' the SED has devised a reliable method of governmental control. For the SED, elections no longer present any sort of problem, they are exclusively a 'means of integration for the strengthening and further development of the socialist power of the state'.[2] The possibility of naming more candidates for election than there are seats, conceded for the first time in the Electoral Law of 1965, has done nothing to change the fact that the function of elections in the GDR is simply to give assent to the system.

4 THE COUNCIL OF STATE

The Council of State is an institution which carries out the 'fundamental tasks' of the People's Chamber between its actual sessions in the same way that the Politbüro of the SED functions between the sessions of the Central Committee, as laid down by the party rules. The Council of State is elected by the People's Chamner. Its first Chairman was Walter Ulbricht, who held this office since the creation of the Council of State in 1960, and who retained this office even after his replacement as First Secretary of the SED by Erich Honecker. After his death in 1973 the post was taken over by Willi Stoph, previously Chairman of the Council of Ministers.

The numerical composition of the Council of State is not specified in the Constitution. This only speaks of the chairman, his deputies, the members and the secretary. At present the Council of State has 24 members 5 of these deputies of the chairman; The chairman of the Council of Ministers is also *ex officio* a member of the Council of State; 15 of the 24 members belong to the SED, of the remainder 2 each to the other block parties. Once again therefore this is no committee composed purely of SED members but rather, as with all state bodies, an institution directed by the SED in the political course it is to take.

The term of office of the Council of State is coupled with the period of legislature of the People's Chamber and is thus four years. The Council of State combines functions of the most different kinds. It can act in situations which, in parliamentary systems, are usually dealt with by the Head of State, and also in those which in our system are dealt with by parliament or the government. In addition, it is also the supreme body in all questions concerning the interpretation of the Constitution and in controlling the administration of justice. The principle of unity of powers or concentration of powers is seen particularly clearly in this institution.

According to the Constitution, the most important functions of the Council of State are as follows:

1. To represent the state abroad: this is done by the Chairman.
2. Dealing with all draft bills laid before the People's Chamber and including the right to tackle its 'fundamental tasks' by making its own legally binding decrees and resolutions.
3. Fixing dates and issuing writs for elections.
4. Fundamental decisions concerning questions of defence and public safety, including the right to pronounce a 'state of emergency'.
5. Testing the constitutionality of draft bills, giving the authorized interpretation of the Constitution and its laws and controlling the constitutionality of the actions of the supreme legal bodies.
6. The right to propose candidates for the chairmanship of the Council of Ministers, for the National Defence Council and for the highest judicial offices.
7. Laying down the agenda for the People's Chamber (if, as is usual, the People's Chamber does not itself do so).

The law-making capacity of the Council of State must be regarded as having special significance. It can both pass decrees—which, admittedly, need formal ratification by the People's Chamber—and also make legally binding resolutions, which do not require specific confirmation. As a rule, these resolutions are used as orders by the Council of State to further the development of the socialist order of society—in other words, they are measures of decisive importance for the system as a whole. Both the law-making capacity of the Council of State as well as the ordinance-issuing capacity of the Council of Ministers (both being forms of delegated legislation) are used in the GDR to an extent going far beyond the ordinance-issuing capacities of governments in western democracies. There is no clearly defined ranking in the authority of the various law-making bodies; in principle the laws (of the People's Chamber) take precedence over the decrees (of the Council of State) and these in turn over the ordinances (of the Council of Ministers). Since, however, there is no body having jurisdiction over administrative and constitutional organs, there is no control over the ranking of the law-making authorities. This also helps to explain why the GDR is able to manage with so few formal laws.

The Council of State has a relatively small bureaucratic apparatus. This is only possible because on the one hand it is closely linked to the government (Council of Ministers) which can supply it with the documents necessary for the preparation of its resolutions, and on the other hand it can draw on the resolutions and prepared bills of the SED party apparatus. Its function as 'guardian of the Constitution' requires no special juridical knowledge since in the GDR as in other socialist states, the law is essentially a function of politics and, as has been said, there is no special jurisdiction over either administrative or constitutional bodies.

It is also worth mentioning that the Council of State is not designated as 'an organ working collectively', in contrast to other state organs in the GDR as, for instance, the Council of Ministers. The Chairman of the Council of State therefore holds a particularly important position which is underlined by the fact that as a rule he is also the First Secretary of the SED. It is greatly strengthened by the further fact that the chairman of the Council of State takes part in all functions which require the personal representation of the state at home and abroad. The Council of State as a whole rarely makes any public appearance.

The construction of the Council of State has been characterized as an institutional ordering of power, specifically tailored for Ulbricht. Nevertheless, it is noteworthy that Erich Honecker as the new First Secretary of the SED obviously does wield greater power than the chairman Walter Ulbricht, who remained as head of the Council of State but had to tolerate certain changes in GDR politics under Honecker. This shows that it is really the SED which rules the country through its First Secretary, in spite of the constitutional powers of the Council of State and its chairman; that the organization of the state is therefore, in the first place, an instrument in the hand of the powerful party. The Politbüro, though having no constitutional functions in the state, is always more powerful than the Council of State, and its chairman is more powerful than the chairman of the Council of State, unless the two offices happen anyway to be held by one man.

Walter Ulbricht, First Secretary of the SED from the beginning until he was succeeded by Erich Honecker, and also Chairman of the Council of State, was the very personification of the SED régime. Just as Adenauer, a Rhinelander, stamped the first 15 years of the Federal Republic with his own personal imprint, so too did Ulbricht, a Saxonian, put his stamp on the first 20 years in the development of the GDR. To a certain extent the GDR is the creation of Walter Ulbricht. Though criticized at the beginning, he became during the sixties the country's 'grand old man'. Without him it is impossible to understand the origins of the GDR and its development into a successful, socialist industrial state, which is still faithful to Moscow.

5 THE COUNCIL OF MINISTERS

The Council of State has been in existence only since 1960 because, although it had been planned by the SED as early as 1949, it was not thought proper to introduce it until the death of Wilhelm Pieck, the first and only State President—this office, restricted only to representational functions, had been a compromise in favour of the bourgeois parties. The Council of Ministers, on the other hand, goes back to the early 1950s without there ever having been any formal change in the Constitution to provide for such alteration. The name Council of Ministers appears for the first time in Acts of 1950 and 1952 taking the place of 'Government of the Republic' which is found in the Constitution. By the Council of Ministers Act of 16 November 1954—later followed by others, the most recent in 1972—the governmental tasks were individually defined. These Acts served as the basis for the rules now dealing with the Council of Ministers in Articles 78–80 of the new Constitution.

The Council of Ministers is elected for a period of 4 years by the newly elected People's Chamber. According to the Constitution, the chairman of the Council of Ministers is appointed by the chairman of the People's Chamber and entrusted with the task of forming the Council of Ministers. In practice, however, it is the Central Committee of the SED which meets before this formal procedure takes place and which is really responsible for forming the Council of Ministers.

The Council of Ministers is indeed no longer a government in the full sense of the word. It must share important governmental functions with the Council of State. The National Defence Council, also set up in 1960, removed from it all important functions with regard to defence and general security. The chairman of the National Defence Council at present is Erich Honecker, First Secretary of the SED.

Clearly, therefore, the Council of Ministers is not the exclusive organ of government but is concerned in a special way with the planning and control of the economy within the framework of government. True, Article 78 states that it must organize the 'political, economic, cultural and social tasks of the socialist state as well as those matters of defence which are assigned to it' but already the second paragraph of the same article specifies: 'The Council of Ministers works out scientifically-based prognoses, organizes the structuring of the economic system of socialism and directs the planned development of the economy'. The authority of the Council of Ministers is, of course, dependent on the laws and resolutions of the People's Chamber, on the basis of which it has to work. In essence the Council of Ministers has to administer the resolutions made by the Council of State, the People's Chamber and the Politbüro.

In the GDR, therefore, the Council of Ministers has virtually no influence on the 'policy guidelines' which, in the Federal German system, are largely determined by the Federal Chancellor as head of the government. It is thus quite consistent for the Council of Ministers to be bound by the Constitution to work collectively, in other words to work according to the cabinet system in which the chairman is simply *primus inter pares*. In a similar way to the Council of State, the chairman of the Council of Ministers has several deputies: there are 2 chief deputy chairmen, 11 deputy chairmen, of whom only 3 at present have their own ministry; only then come the ministers who are responsible for their own particular departments, as stated by the Constitution. Of these there are about 30 because the ministerial structure is far more differentiated than in western governmental systems, being more in accordance with that of the Soviet Union.

The Council of Ministers is a relatively large body consisting of over 40 persons which in turn necessitates the setting up of a controlling committee in the shape of a 'presidency of the Council of Ministers'. In essence this presidency consists of the chairman and his numerous deputies. Those deputies who have no ministry of their own—which is the majority—correspond approximately to ministers without portfolio: they either have specific tasks of co-ordination or special mandates.

For the Council of Ministers as a whole, its law-making capacity is limited to the enactment of orders; for individual ministers to the enactment of regulations and administrative rules for carrying out the legally binding decrees of the other organs. Amongst these must be included the decrees of the Central Committee of the SED in so far as they concern the activities of the state. From this it is clear that the decrees of the leading party are also directly binding on the apparatus of state, without requiring any intervention from other organs of state such as the People's Chamber or the Council of State.

Over the course of years, the organization of the supreme state administration in the GDR has undergone a series of changes which it does not seem necessary to mention in detail. Changes in the structure of ministries and the state offices, as for instance the State Planning Commission, which are equal in rank to the ministries, are of course frequent, where the government itself is concerned with efficiency of administration. The large number of specialist ministries (about 12) in the fields of economics and industry shows the pre-eminence given to the economic tasks of state in the organizational framework. For example, there is a Ministry for Production Machinery and Vehicle Building, in addition to a Ministry for the Chemical Industry and so on. Cultural affairs are similarly subdivided. Apart from a Ministry of Culture, there is a Minister for Elementary Education, a Minister for Higher and Vocational Education as well as a Minister for Science and Technology.

Such ministerial organization is also an indication of the special priorities in state activities: these are in the fields of industry and the economy and in the fields of science and education. Of course there also has to be a Ministry of Defence and ministries for Foreign Affairs, Home Affairs and Justice, the classical departments. This fan-like structure of ministries makes the task of co-ordination an important one for the Council of Ministers and, indeed, one that is demanded by the Constitution.

6 THE ORGANIZATION OF ADMINISTRATION

The GDR is a centrally administered state. Not only the organization of the party and the other political bodies but also the structure of the state is in accordance with the principles of democratic centralism. As early as 1952 the 5 *Länder* of the eastern zone had to yield to this principle; previously, even after the Constitution of 1949, they had still been linked to the central state authority under a federal system—that is, they still possessed their own sovereignty and safeguarded their interests by means of a *Länderkammer*, parallel to the People's Chamber and comparable in composition to the Federal German *Bundesrat*. In 1952, however, these *Länder* were obliged, in the course of 'further democratization of the structure and *modus operandi* of the state organs' to prepare a territorial reorganization and abolish themselves. This reform led to the formation of 14 districts (excluding East Berlin) out of the 5 *Länder* which, to simplify matters, were named after the main city in each. Today the GDR has the following districts: Schwerin, Rostock, Neubrandenburg, Potsdam, Frankfurt an der Oder, Cottbus, Magdeburg, Halle, Erfurt, Gera, Suhl, Dresden, Leipzig and Karl-Marx-Stadt (formerly Chemnitz). The tasks previously undertaken by the organs of the *Länder* were transferred from 1952 to the new districts. At the same time a reorganization of regions (*Kreise*) took place, in which the economic aspect was one of the main criteria taken into account. The *Länderkammer* remained in existence for a time (until 1958) but the reorganization of administrative units on GDR territory had created the pre-conditions for the organization of a centrally-controlled state administration. This allowed its subdivision (districts, areas, cities and communities) no further share of their former autonomy in specific fields of public administration. Today the GDR is a state with central administration in which regional or local administration has autonomy only within a very narrow framework of laws, made by the central state. A specially set up ministry 'for the direction and control of district and regional councils' underlines the virtual absence of any decision-making authority amongst provincial and communal organs.

The Constitution of the GDR classifies the subdivisions of the administrative structure of the state as 'local representation and its bodies'. In all branches of state administration there is an elected representative body at district, regional, city and community level. All these representative bodies in their turn must elect a council and standing committee to act as executive; these must work collectively and make use of special committees formed by the representative bodies for specific tasks. The councils possess no autonomy but are responsible to the Council of Ministers and the higher councils. Altogether there are in the GDR, below the level of the 15 districts (including East Berlin), 214 regional councils (*Kreistage*) as well as about 9000 local bodies in the cities and communes.

The Constitution specially emphasizes the necessity of the organized co-operation of the people in the structuring of public life as well as in the task of 'constantly improving working and living conditions for the people' and increasing their 'awareness of the socialist state and justice'. This is intended to ensure that the state bodies at all levels see their function as a democratic one and that each works towards the creation and further development of the socialist society in its own field.

Officials in the old traditional German sense of that word no longer exist in the GDR. All civil service posts have been brought into line with the rights of workers in general and the special legal rights and social position of official 'state servants' have come to an end. Because of the unity of state and society this is a logical step. There is no convincing proof that the abolition of the 'traditional bases of the civil service' still contained in the West German Basic Law, have led to any lessening in the quality of public service in the GDR. Naturally the idea of a politically neutral civil service is irrelevant in the GDR because its party allegiance is now a political principle.

1. Böckenförde, E. W., *Die Rechtsauffassung im kommunistischen Staat* (Munich 1967), 60.
2. ibid., 65.

5 | The legal system

The concept of permanent principles underlying the law, such as is found in western legal history perhaps most significantly in the idea of Natural Law, is totally alien to socialist thinking. Marxism sees the law only as having a concrete social function. Accordingly each era in social development has its own code of law corresponding to and based upon the underlying socio-economic conditions. Seen in Marxist terms, all law is class-dependent and always expresses in its material content the dominance of a particular class. One must therefore see the socialist legal code of the GDR as expressing the dominance of the working classes which, according to the Constitution of 1968, possess all power in state and society.

True, the legal system in a socialist state is not simply the manifestation of changed social and economic conditions, not simply a superstructure in the sense that Marx and Engels regarded the law as being superimposed on the conditions of production which determine historical development. The law is also an instrument of social practice and to this extent a means of consciously transforming society in a socialist sense. 'Socialist Law absorbs the objective principles of the socialist society and thus acts as a lever for their deliberate enforcement.'[1] This lever-effect gives the legal system a formative function in accordance with the objective principles established by the ruling party; in other words, the law is not so much a means for safeguarding order and existing conditions but rather a means of further developing the socialist society. The law of 1963 on the Administration of Justice which also deals with basic questions of socialist justice, therefore states: 'Socialist law is an important instrument of our state for the organization of social development.'

It follows from this that the GDR, like other socialist systems, regards the legal system principally as a tool of politics. Political life and the organs of the Executive, especially the leading socialist party, are not restricted or held in check by socialist law but, on the contrary, the law is an instrument for the enforcement of their political views.

The law thus has no independence which would justify the separation of judicial power from law-making and executive powers, neither is there any distinction between law and politics. 'The socialist administration of law is not an independent "pillar" of power, separated from other parts of the apparatus of state; but—within the social and state organism which in its totality embodies the political and common interests of all workers—it is a specific form of state and social activity serving to safeguard, protect and advance those rights of the people and that observance of modes of behaviour declared to be obligatory in the common interest and embodied in the Constitution and the laws.'[2]

The ideological background and instrumental character of the law in the socialist democracy of the GDR is already apparent on a purely superficial level, in that a large number of the articles of the 1968 Constitution are programmatic in nature; it is also seen in the fact that those laws passed by the People's Chamber are generally provided with extensive preambles. These serve to express in detail the ideological bases of the law and the particularity of the socio-economic development of the socialist society to which they give expression; further they are aids for juridical interpretation, which thus makes it possible to dispense largely with formal legal training.

In western legal systems it is the very formality of the law and the legal system which plays a vital part; therefore problems concerning the processes of justice, the due process of law and the formal ranking of legal decisions have an important function. They are, indeed, occasionally even identified with the principle of the constitutional state. Such formal problems are of very subordinate character in the law of the GDR. There is no clear system of ranking or of defining the authority of the various sources of law; there are no independent judicial bodies, which can keep a check on the legality of acts of the state, moreover the relative constancy and reliability of legal authorities which are well known in bourgeois constitutional states do not exist.

Since the law is principally utilitarian in character it is mainly subject, in both interpretation and application, to the influence of the political authorities which determine its material content. To this extent socialist law lacks those categories, so essential to the bourgeois state, namely certainty, stability and predictability. In the view of 'socialist law', the interpretation of legal statutes, be it the Constitution or legislation, is not chiefly a question of legal dogma of concern to jurists, but rather a question of political expediency of concern to politicians. For this reason too it is the Council of State and not some legal body which has the final word in interpreting the Constitution and the law.

The legal system of the GDR in its present form proceeds from the socialist society as an established fact. Since (so it is argued) socialist society is determined by its own basic values and does not suffer from that antagonism so typical of bourgeois society, its legal concepts can be given a 'qualitatively new content' even if these concepts are often couched in identical terms to those of the bourgeois state. As the official commentary to Article 86 of the Constitution, which introduces the section on 'Socialist legislation and administration of justice', puts it, socialism implies the renewal of all human values and brings about the development of completely new living conditions and a new morality.

In a socialist society having man as its focal point, the law is not only a means for involving each citizen in the socialist community but also an instrument of education. Unlike those bourgeois legal systems which simply establish an 'ethical minimum', the law has an important moral aspect. This is further underlined in the organization of the legal system by a deliberate involvement of social organizations in the processes of law. Thus the law as a whole helps the political powers towards a better development of the socialist society which is their goal, by being the expression of 'socialist law'; at the same time, it applies to the individual citizen principally by helping him to develop into a 'socialist personality with a new set of moral, cultural and intellectual needs and ideals'.[3]

Socialist law, therefore, is not a system conceived primarily for the preservation of individual interests, as is essentially true of the legal systems of liberal bourgeois societies; it is, rather, social law, a legal system for the community. As the GDR sees it, the legal system as a whole exists to serve the general interests of the socialist community and simultaneously, to help each individual citizen find his own place within it. As is continually stressed, it is the *common* interests and aims of all the people which are embodied in socialist law, and not the rights of individuals. This emphasis on common interests and the community in socialist law necessarily points to an authority which will formulate these common aims and interests in a legally binding manner. In the socialist society of the GDR this authority can only be the leading party of the ruling working classes, the SED.

2 THE BASIC RIGHTS

The special features of the legal system of the socialist GDR, compared with those western democracies, cast in the mould of the bourgeois constitutional state, are seen not least in its conception of basic rights and their function. In western theories of the state, basic rights are commonly regarded as individual freedoms which the state has to respect. A developed socialist society, as the GDR regards itself, likewise has basic rights and attaches great importance to them in the theory of law, yet on account of the different social conditions, basic rights in the socialist system do not have the same meaning as in bourgeois society. They are not rights against the state; they do not guarantee a private, protected sphere for the individual but rather act in an integrating capacity by ensuring that the individual participates in the life of the state. In the communist view, a society that is free of all antagonism does not need to safeguard a free sphere for the individual as against the state but can proceed from a consensus of opinion on political, material and cultural matters amongst all sections of society. The basic rights are the detailed expression of the individual citizen's demand for participation in all the various areas of social life. For this reason the 'right of co-determination and collaboration' (Art. 21) is seen as the fundamental basic right of socialism. The socialist state believes that it has laid the economic and political foundations for ensuring a real participation of all citizens in shaping their society. This is guaranteed for them by the basic rights.

The nature of the socialist basic rights, which aim at integrating the individual into the social and political order, is further underlined by another feature of the socialist legal system, namely by a strong emphasis on basic duties as the necessary complement to basic rights. In the legal theory of the GDR, rights and duties form an inseparable unit. The acceptance of certain civic duties as the norm—for instance the duty to work, the duty to be educated—is the practical complement to the corresponding basic rights. 'The socialist basic rights involve the obligation to put them actively into practice, since this alone guarantees their existence and their development.'[4]

The new function of basic rights in the constitutional system of the GDR has also led to a change of emphasis in the theory of basic rights. Instead of emphasizing the right of individual freedom as in the West, it is the right of participation which stands well to the fore in the socialist system, namely:

1. the right and duty of social and political participation;
2. the right and duty to work, since only involvement in the social process of work can enable man to fulfil his productive potential; finally
3. the right and duty of education: by means of education the individual can participate in the general cultural process and develop his intellectual capacity: this then enables him to give of his best within the social productive process.

Thus the basic rights are, on the one hand, integrating factors and as such, on the other hand, they guarantee social welfare and protection. It is, above all, this social aspect of the basic rights which is also gaining increasing importance in western industrial societies.

Both basic rights and basic duties, of course, relate solely to the socialist form of society and are effective only therein. Any activity against the socialist order is therefore impossible as a basic right, neither is any indifference to society protected as such. All this means that the basic rights simply confirm what the state desires of its citizens, namely their active collaboration for the common good.

In the legal system of the GDR the juridical protection of the individual is of subordinate importance, for both constitutional and legal theory proceeds from the fact that the political, economic and ideological conditions for human development have already been created in the GDR and do not first have to be effectively safeguarded by the verdict of a court of law. In legal proceedings the individual citizen cannot resort to basic rights. They therefore play a very minor role in legal matters. To safeguard the rights of the citizen, the Constitution simply allows him to file petitions with the elected bodies, which are, of course, political organizations, The unity of powers permits no investigation by an independent court of law.

3 STAGES IN THE DEVELOPMENT OF THE LEGAL SYSTEM OF THE GDR

The Constitution of 1946 which remained in force until the second Constitution of 1968 was not socialist in character but bourgeois and democratic and largely modelled on the Constitution of the Weimar Republic of 1919, with a few concessions to socialist constitutional theory. The main concession was the principle of unity of powers. Admittedly a considerable number of individual articles were in conflict with it, yet in conjunction with block politics this principle proved to be the real lever in bringing about a socialist order of state and society. The second important concession to the future development of a socialist constitution was the planning of the economy which accepted the restriction of private ownership as the norm. This created the conditions necessary for introducing a wholly planned economy and for a shift in ownership ratio away from individuals and in favour of the socialist state.

Since—in the Marxist view—a legal system corresponds to its underlying social and economic conditions, the Constitution of 1949 obviously could not be such a fully developed socialist constitution as that of 1968. Rather, the conditions for the development of a social order had first to be created one by one, before the written Constitution could become the expression of such an order.

In practice this meant that the Constitution of 1949 possessed only little legal force and that many of its articles were superseded by conflicting laws and acts of state, so that a West German constitutional lawyer has said of it: 'The Constitution which is "actually" in force is largely only a *de facto* constitution and not a legally valid one. The "formally valid" Constitution lacks the power of enforcement in reality and actual constitutional practice lacks legal validity.'[5]

Such a judgement is, of course, put forward entirely from a western viewpoint, for the decisions made by the Party Conferences of the SED, its Central Committee, its Council of Ministers and later its Council of State certainly did have legally binding force in the GDR, even if they appeared to contradict the actual wording of the 1949 Constitution. The text of the 1949 Constitution itself was altered only three times in all, in 1955 for the introduction of military service, in 1958 for the abolition of the *Länderkammer* (i.e. State Assemblies) and finally in 1960 for the creation of the Council of State in place of the President of the Republic. However, a series of laws successively weakened the power of the Constitution on many points until it finally resulted in that political state of affairs which was codified in the new Constitution of 1968.

The jurisprudence of the GDR has covered actual constitutional changes by extensive interpretation. Since there is no Constitutional Court, any contradiction between a law and the Constitution would be impossible to settle. Also in the various branches of law, such as civil, criminal and economic law, the GDR had first to make do with such traditional bases of law as for instance, the Civil Code. In the course of its progressive transformation into a socialist state, however, it systematically tackled the new codification of these various branches of law: it created a new Criminal Code, a new Family Law and a new Industrial Law; it is now on the point of reformulating and reorganizing what remains as Civil Law. In short it is transforming existing law into an instrument of social change as dictated by the political aims of the SED, frequently by contradicting its original meaning, by a convenient reinterpretation of existing regulations or with the help of broadly phrased general clauses. From the outset the state made use of so-called 'People's Judges' who were sufficiently reliable politically to interpret the law according to the ideological principles of socialism without too many legal subtleties. In this way 'socialist law' evolved step by step, and is now laid down in the relevant articles of the new Constitution.

The development of the socialist legal system of the GDR can be divided into various periods of time which can be seen as stages on the way to a fully formed socialist system of laws. The first phase, beginning immediately after the founding of the state and giving political expression to the transformation of the SED into a new type of party, coincides with the SED taking complete control of state power and with the internal and external safeguarding of the 'power of the working classes'. During this phase the state made use of the law, subordinated to politics, primarily as a means of repressing the former ruling class, which it defeated by class warfare. At this time the fight against all real and supposed enemies of the new order was of prime importance as far as justice was concerned: they were prosecuted as 'enemies of the [working] classes' and rendered 'harmless'.

The second stage, which can be roughly dated between 1957 and 1963, is the phase of transition from the 'dictatorship of the proletariat' or, rather, the system of 'people's democracy' to the developed socialist society. By now the power of state had become well established and could therefore deal consistently with the construction and legal organization of a planned socialist order. During this phase the legal system had the special task of creating the right legal conditions for carrying out the economic and other administrative tasks of state. The last and current phase in which the socialist democracy is to be perfected and which is subject to the law of 'socialist jurisdiction' corresponds to the all-embracing establishment of socialism, proclaimed by both party and constitution. In this stage of development the law no longer has the primary function of being an instrument of state politics—it is at the same time also an instrument of social policy. This new trend in the administration of justice is recognizable by its tendency to set up community courts as well as by its emphasis on the educational tasks of the law, which sees it and its institutions not so much as an instrument of repression against potential enemies of the working classes but rather as a means of linking man with his society. This stage emphasizes a new quality in law, namely its complete conformity with the interests of all citizens. Thus, it is claimed, the law is not in opposition to the citizen as is so often the case in the bourgeois state, but the socialist system of law expresses the will of the people and they themselves are therefore the guarantors of 'socialist law'.

4 SOCIALIST LAW

There are two main points necessary for an understanding of socialist law. Firstly the legal system must be seen and interpreted from the standpoint of the 'developed social system of socialism'. This means that it regulates in a legally-binding form 'the basic social relationships of its citizens and in particular the very important relationships between citizen and community and again between both these and the state'.[6] Socialist law is seen as the expression of the political will of the working classes, for 'under their leadership together with that of the Marxist-Leninist party Socialism becomes a reality'.[7] Secondly, in order to become reality, socialist law requires 'the involvement of both citizen and community in the administration of law' (Art. 87). This participation of the people in the administration of law is seen as 'the most significant way of exercising political power and, at the same time, of social self-education by the working classes'.[8]

Socialist law is the socialist equivalent of the bourgeois concept of a constitutional state. It is true that the socialist concept of law also emphasizes an obligatory strict observance of rules of law, thus expressing the need for legal obligations and safeguards. However, since these rules of law are always seen in conjunction with 'the objective requirements of social development', they are not as restrictive and limiting as in western democracies. Admittedly in the western democratic system, too, the law is seen as the expression of the political will of the people, since it is codified by democratically elected assemblies, also the law is administered 'in the name of the people'. Nevertheless, once the law has been codified, it is entrusted solely to the judiciary and thus removed from direct influence by political bodies. Furthermore its interpretation is not influenced by being ideologically linked with the state of social development. This link between socialist law and socialist politics, seen also in the actual organization of justice, is the main distinction between the socialist system of law and the western concept of the constitutional state.

This special feature of the socialist legal system is already expressed in the enactment of the law. The Constitution, the fundamental document of the state, is characterized by the dominance of general principles which are hardly comprehensible from a juridical standpoint. Thus, for instance, the first article of the section on 'Socialist law and the administration of justice' (Art. 86) says: 'Socialist society, the political power of the working classes and their organization of state and law are the basic guarantee for the [terms of the] Constitution being observed and realized in the spirit of justice, equality, brotherliness and humanity'. Commentaries on the Constitution in the GDR do not attempt to give precise juridical expression to the terms of the Constitution, but are, as a rule, verbose paraphrases of the decrees, with ideological and historical arguments taking precedence over juridical analyses.

The legal statutes of the GDR are also frequently a framework for provisions which are only given concrete shape by orders and directives issued by the executive and only thus do they attain actual legal force. Moreover, the codification of law in the GDR generally makes intensive use of indefinite legal concepts and general clauses, which can then be interpreted by the courts according to political expediency. Thus, for instance, Article 6 of the old Constitution (against incitement to boycott) was the general legal basis for the extensive political persecutions of the Stalinist era in the GDR. In addition the preambles to the laws of the GDR always contain a mass of general political principles (e.g. the law serves to strengthen socialist democracy etc.) which are intended to suggest what its interpretation should be and which, on account of their purely political character, in their turn reveal the dependence of law on politics. Finally, not all legal rules are valid in the same way: the bodies concerned with the administration of justice are advised from time to time to emphasize particular points, in other words to take special note of certain legal rules whilst ignoring others. Since in any case all judges are bound by the principle of party allegiance in giving judgement—which means that they must help to put into practice the decrees of the party and the state organs subordinate to it— it is impossible in practice for the judiciary to be set apart from the political bodies. It is an established fact that in the GDR justice is an instrument of politics.

A limited amount of independence for the judicial bodies may

D

be seen solely in the fact that in a decision of 1967, the Supreme Court established that it was illegal to give an interpretation of the law which contradicted its plain meaning. This has limited complete arbitrariness in interpretation, yet because of the juridical imprecision of many statutes, this remnant of independence for the 'third power' can have little effect in the face of direct intervention in legal decisions. It is clear that the GDR, within the framework of its concept of socialist law, is concerned more strongly than before with preserving and safeguarding the law. This too is an expression of its inner consolidation.

5 THE ORGANIZATION OF JUSTICE

Significantly enough the Constitution of the GDR no longer speaks of the law and its organs but classifies the entire legal system as *administration of justice*. This is intended to show that the law is not simply a means in the hands of the state of settling conflicts but is, above all, an instrument for realizing and perfecting the socialist society. Because the law is a tool and a support of politics it requires constant attention and the active participation of the people. In the words of the Constitution (Art. 90) the administration of justice serves the practical execution of socialist law and the protection and development of the GDR and its state and social order.

The administrative organs of justice function within a socialist state ruled by a single political power. Because the law has no independent power but has to express the political will of the working classes, it is consistent with the terms of socialist logic if the professional and lay judges as well as the members of the so-called Community Courts are elected or appointed by the political bodies at the various levels and are then responsible to them. The judges of the Supreme Court are appointed by the People's Chamber, those of the district courts by the district assemblies and so forth. The judges of the Community Courts are appointed by works assemblies and housing associations. Like all other elected political representatives, judges can be dismissed. Although judges are guaranteed some independence even by the Constitution of the GDR (Art. 96) and are bound by law and statute, the possibility of dismissal is not excluded. The fact that independence does not preclude dismissal as in the bourgeois constitutional state, is explained by saying that only those judges can be wholly independent who possess the confidence of the people. The principle of non-dismissability contradicts the idea of sovereignty of the people; it is thus a bourgeois principle which protects the judge from exercising his democratic responsibility towards the people. Since, in the political system of the GDR, the 'confidence of the people' is defined solely by the leading party, this interpretation of the principle of judicial independence again reveals that the judiciary is in fact politically dependent.

Within the legal system the principle of democratic centralism is just as evident as in the party and the organs of state. The highest judicial body is the Supreme Court which is responsible to the People's Chamber and the Council of State. The Constitution states that it 'directs' the judgements of the courts and ensures uniformity in the execution of justice. Directing judgements means that the Supreme Court can give the lower courts (at district and area level) 'obligatory indications' for the execution of justice. This is to ensure that all courts in the GDR apply laws and other legal regulations 'uniformly and correctly'. This directive function goes far beyond that of supreme courts in western systems. There the supreme courts only suggest how the law should be interpreted in the light of concrete decisions; they do not give legally binding indications to the lower courts as to how specific questions of law should be dealt with.

The Supreme Court carries out its directive function chiefly by means of its plenary session which is its highest body. To this belong the chairmen of the 15 regional courts and the higher military courts in addition to all the professional judges. Another function of the Supreme Court is to make suggestions to the Council of State on the interpretation of specific laws and it can instigate the changing or abolition of legal decrees. It reports on its activities to the Council of State at periodic intervals.

There are three types of judges in the legal administration of the GDR: 1) professional judges; 2) lay judges and 3) the members of the Community Courts. Only the professional judges need to have qualifications. Lay judges or assessors have the same rights as professional judges; their appointment depends solely on their social qualifications. These are determined by two factors (a knowledge of the law is only taken into account in the case of professional judges): 1) a knowledge of 'the legal principles of social development' which are, of course, ideological and 2) a capacity for understanding the thoughts and feelings of the people, which is, of course, collectivist.[9]

Numerically, too, lay judges play a very important part in the administration of justice; many tribunals have only one professional judge as chairman and two lay judges who have equal rights. The lay judges hold office for two weeks at a time and then return to their jobs. Altogether approximately 50 000 men and women act as lay judges during the year, compared with 1200 full-time professional judges. This proportion is seen as an expression of the 'growing unity between the people and the administration of justice'.

6 THE COMMUNITY COURTS

The so-called Community Courts are another special feature of the administration of law in the GDR. There are two different kinds: *Konfliktkommissionen* (industrial tribunals) in firms and industries and *Schiedskommissionen* (arbitration tribunals) in housing estates. The industrial tribunals were already set up in 1953 to settle labour disputes; the arbitration tribunals were not introduced until 10 years later. Both have been entrusted since 1963 with making legally binding judicial decisions. By means of the Community Courts the people have a direct share in giving judgement; also the primary task of the Community Courts is the moral education of the people in the interests of the collective good. Moreover they relieve the judicial apparatus of the state of many small disputes; they are already seen as a preliminary stage in the lessening of state power which is one of the final aims of Marxist ideology. The members of the Community Courts as well as the lay judges acting as assessors in the state courts are supposed to be exemplary in their personal behaviour, which means that their political and moral qualifications are an essential requirement for their appointment. Since there are no professionally-trained judges in the Community Courts, the Minister of Justice sees to the essential juridical instruction of the members of the courts in the case of arbitration tribunals; in the case of the industrial tribunals which concentrate primarily on questions of labour law, the Federation of Trades Unions has undertaken the relevant training for the members.

Even amongst the group of professional judges the state has succeeded in breaking the former predominance of those with a middle-class background who as a rule are still found in the West. According to official sources in the GDR[10] over two thirds of professional judges come from working-class families and of these almost one third are women. Women also account for 40% of the lay judges.

However one may rate the quality of justice in the GDR, it cannot be disputed that to a certain extent the GDR has succeeded in integrating the process of law into the social system by engaging lay people in it. In the proceedings of the state courts, too, especially with criminal proceedings, social groups are represented in the shape of social prosecuting and defence lawyers in order to present the social 'basis' regarding the case in question. Naturally arguments are, as a rule, in line with an attitude to society and the function of the individual within it based on Marxist-Leninist ideology; nevertheless the process of law serves, in this way, not only to pass sentence or to give judgement but is also a forum for the development and application of a socialist morality. To what extent the organization of the administration of justice has really become a means for collective self-education and individual education cannot be reliably assessed. It is certain that the involvement of the community in the process of law can counteract a bureaucratic and conceptual isolation of the juridical apparatus from the other spheres of the state and of society. Already today one third of all criminal cases are heard by the Community Courts and in the great majority of cases, the arbitration and industrial tribunals succeed in bringing about an acceptable settlement between the parties concerned. An appeal to the ordinary courts is always open to them.

The strong involvement of social groups in the processes of law expresses the conviction that the conflicts and disputes so typical of bourgeois society decrease in the developed socialist society according to its degree of perfection, and, indeed, finally disappear altogether. The great historical process which is the evolution of the socialist community of man, so it is said, leaves increasingly less opportunity for any thought or activity in opposition to society. Since all bases for antagonism have been removed there must be a decreasing tendency to offend against socialist law and fewer cases of law-breaking.

If, in spite of all this, crime still exists in the GDR it is, on the one hand, a relic of old, traditional habits stemming from the capitalist era, and on the other hand it is connected with the harmful ideological influences of imperialism, still affecting the present time, and with 'criminal activities against the social order directly organized by imperialist powers'.[11]

The belief in a gradual decrease of state justice as a means of social discipline and repression reflects a utopian image of Marxist eschatology, the idea of socialist man living beyond all oppression in the realm of true freedom and where classes and conflicts no longer exist. The ideologists of the GDR really believe that in the course of socialist development the law will increasingly fulfil a sort of confirmatory social function and will be able to recede into the background as a means of deciding conflicts and passing sentence on offenders. The administration of justice is thus more than giving judgement: it aims at grafting socialist law and morality more firmly into the minds and behavioural patterns of its citizens. This aim, admittedly, is hard to achieve. It is therefore impossible, now as always, for the political rulers to dispense with the legal system as a servant of their own claims to power.

1. 'Thesen zum Wesen und zur Entwicklung des sozialistischen Rechts', *Staat und Recht,* 1963, 1842 ff.
2. *Kommentar zur DDR-Verfassung* (Berlin 1969), vol. 2, 428.
3. ibid., 407.
4. ibid., 13.
5. Drath, M., in Mampel, S., *Die Sozialistische Verfassung der DDR* (Frankfurt 1972). Text and commentary.
6. *Kommentar,* vol. 2, 409.
7. ibid., 409.
8. ibid., 411.
9. ibid., 452.
10. ibid., 455.
11. ibid., 430.

6 | Social structure and politics

Despite all official pronouncements, the actual constitution of society in the GDR is complex rather than homogeneous, fragile rather than stable, contradictory rather than harmonious. Although the undertaking is difficult, however, we shall attempt to sketch some of the characteristics essential for an understanding of this society and to examine the factors which bring about these characteristics and the changes affecting them.

The first factor in any analysis of society and its politics is man in his demographic aspect. Of the wealth of data regarding the structure of the population as given by the Bonn government in the *Materialien zum Bericht zur Lage der Nation* (Data for the report on the state of the nation) of 1971, two aspects have been selected which are fundamental to such an understanding: the general development of the population and its age structure.

The population of the GDR decreased from about 18·8 millions in 1949 to a little over 17 millions in 1971. This serious decrease came about partly because of a considerable drop in the birth rate, but was in the first place a result of a massive flight to the West in the years up to 1961. Only in the two years immediately after the building of the Wall was there a small increase in population; thereafter the statistics again show a decrease. Altogether, in the years between 1948 and 1960, the GDR lost almost 2·7 million people through emigration and this number would have been higher, had it not been counter-balanced by the immigration of people from the former eastern German provinces during the first few years of this period.[1]

The number of refugees from the GDR during these years reflects its political and social development: it was highest in 1953, the year of the people's revolt and the beginning of collective farming, then receded and rose to a new maximum in 1960–1 when the measures for the transfer of agriculture and trade to co-operatives were intensified and the 'closure of the state frontier' was threatened. The enormous loss of population in itself would have been sufficient to pose great problems for the economy of any state, but in the case of the GDR they were greatly intensified by the type of person fleeing the country. Every year up to the building of the Wall about half of all refugees were young people under 25. Amongst adult refugees, too, those of working age predominated; in addition to numerous farmers and skilled craftsmen, the GDR also lost a considerable part of its intelligentsia. Thus the refugee movement worsened the already unfavourable age-structure of the population. Today almost 40% of the population are under 15 or over 65 and therefore do not constitute part of the labour force of the country. These are serious demographic conditions for the economic and social policies of any state and furthermore they are not easily changed since this age-structure necessarily affects the birth rate. In the GDR the inevitable consequence of this situation was to draw on its potential of women and retired people for its work force. East German society will still be affected for many years to come by a lack of workpeople and will therefore need to make use of all reserves at its disposal.

In addition to these demographic facts, the social policies of socialism are the second determining factor in actual East German society. In contrast to the more conservative social policy of western states, that of the socialist states is characterized by a definite concept of social restructuring. This policy is guided by the image of a 'new society' and sees all measures it must take in the present as steps towards such a future. As is well known, the teachings and policies of Marxism and Leninism are aimed at the creation of a communist society in which, according to Marx's famous dictum, 'instead of classes and class contrasts there will be an association in which the free development of every individual will be the condition for the free development of all'. The differences between the classes, depending on the possession or non-possession of material goods are to be abolished; there is only to be the unity of all workers who themselves take decisions on their own work which is the means of production.

In Marxist theory, this aim of a communist society cannot be accomplished in a single act of revolution. Between the capitalist and the communist era there has to be a transitional society, a form of socialist society still having the 'hereditary characteristics' of the old capitalist society but already bearing within it the seeds of the new communist society. The social policies of socialism have the task of gradually causing all signs of the old order to disappear and of helping the new to full fruition.

Since all political, social, juridical and cultural conditions are, in Marxist theory, directly attributable to the prevailing production conditions, social policies in socialist states are aimed primarily at changing the structure of ownership. The conversion of the means of production from private to public ownership was therefore the central policy in the GDR both socially and economically, until well into the 1960s. It began during the era of occupation with the expropriation of the large landowners and large-scale industries, continued with the taking over of smaller firms right up to the collectivization of farming and the—still only partially complete—combining of trades into production co-operatives. All these measures have created not only a new economic but also a new social order. In contrast to the former social structure whole classes have disappeared and new social groups been created. Thus, for instance, in 1971 only 0·2% of those engaged in gainful work practised their professions as doctors, engineers, architects, lawyers and the like outside the state system, and even with these it can be foreseen how soon they will be integrated into, for example, socialist assemblies of lawyers or directly into a public combine. The number of independent tradesmen, one-man businesses and innkeepers has increasingly diminished, their place having been taken by members of production and consumer co-operatives as well as by employees of the state trade organizations. Together with those in the agricultural workers' and trade co-operatives they form new groups in the social statistics of the GDR and account for over 11% of those in active employment.

The aim of the socialist policy in the GDR, however, is not simply the external but also the inner transformation of society. A 'socialist community of man' is to arise, in which human relationships are to take on a wholly new quality. The public and private sphere, social and individual interests, rights and duties—all are to fuse into one. Society which was formerly divided into classes is to be integrated into a community of 'socialist personalities'. It is this end which the constant political and social propaganda and socialist education in all spheres of life and all institutions from kindergarten, school and house-community to place of work are there to serve. Everywhere a new socialist morality is preached and practised, a morality intended to overcome the individualism of a bourgeois past and create new, collective forms of living, in which 'I' is to be absorbed into 'we'.

Is it then true to say that a socialist society has arisen in the GDR which differs clearly from both its national and bourgeois past and, even more, from its capitalist neighbour, the Federal Republic? Many impressions and reports from the GDR seem to suggest that its society is less a socialist society in the ideological sense than a strange mixture of German social tradition and the universal tendencies of an industrial society. Both elements have been consciously absorbed by the GDR and made to serve the socialist state order. For this reason it is difficult to ascertain how much is specifically socialist and how much is attributable to causes other than political and ideological ones.

Like all other modern societies, that of the GDR should be seen as a highly complex contradictory social phenomenon. Many and divers factors—the beginnings in the spheres of population and the economy, the roots reaching into German social traditions, the restructuring by the political system and the developments in technology and industry—all these have affected it and affect it still, to interact with each other, set up contradictory forces and thus bring about social change. East German society is no more complete and static than other societies, despite the official portrait of a 'socialist society' with all its artificial harmonies and its all-embracing pseudo-consistency.

2 THE WORKERS—A RULING CLASS?

The characteristic interaction of official interpretations and actual social trends becomes immediately apparent on studying that class which has allegedly taken over the ruling role in the GDR—the working class.

The GDR calls itself a 'state of industrial and agricultural workers', the first German state ruled not by capitalists but by the workers themselves. The actual rule of the workers is to become possible to the extent by which all workers become more qualified and more capable of not simply carrying out production but rather of planning and managing it for themselves. The premise inherent in such rule is therefore that in a socialist state, work as a human activity must take on a different quality from that in a capitalist state: in the latter—so it is maintained—it is characterized by exploitation and the dichotomy between physical and intellectual activity, whereas in socialism it becomes a highly qualified activity in which finally all participants, whether workers or intelligentsia, grow closer together and accept their historically new function as socialist members of a single uniform class to whom everything belongs.

The essential pre-condition for this rule by the working classes is the taking over of all means of production as public property. Today this has been largely fulfilled with the 'victory of socialist production conditions'. Theoretically, therefore, nothing would seem to stand in the way of self-determination by the workers. It is noteworthy that in the economic and social order of the GDR it must be a case of *self-* and not merely *co-*determination. For co-determination would imply that the workers would have their say in addition to others, whereas the whole point is that, by the nationalization of the means of production, they themselves have become the sole owners of it. The term 'co-determination' is therefore avoided in the GDR: the preferred description for the workers' right of participation is 'collaboration'.

Collaboration in shaping the process of production is not simply a right of which any worker may avail himself or not, as he pleases. As a result of nationalization he is not only employee and wage-earner, but also—as we should say—employer and owner. His rights therefore imply duties, arising out of his co-ownership of what is public property. Anyone who neglects his duties in the socialist production process or who misuses his rights, does not offend against a contract with an employer, but harms common property and thereby injures his own interests. Those rights which arise out of the fact of public property for each employee are therefore identical with duties, the primary one being that of increased productivity.

Nowhere is the equation of rights and duties, so characteristic of the whole legal system of the GDR, seen so clearly as in labour law. Thus, the statute book of 12 April 1961 (GBA) dealing with labour law puts, immediately after the *right* to work, the '*duty* to keep a socialist working discipline amongst all workers engaged in the common task, and especially to protect and increase that which belongs to all'.[2] Workers in the GDR are constantly reminded that work is not simply a matter of earning a living, but a 'matter of honour and renown'. It is an honour to be co-owner of public property, and it is laudable to have a share in the progress of the first German workers' state.

What concrete rights of collaboration does the individual worker have over and beyond the fundamental right of recognizing his duties and gladly availing himself of them? To collaborate in planning and management certainly does not mean that the workers in any concern possess autonomous control over 'their concern'. The concerns which have been nationalized have not come into the possession of those actually working in them, but into the possession of the totality of all workers and thus into the control of the state as a whole.

This is also seen in the organizational structure and decision-making of the publicly owned concerns which, like all socialist organizations, follow the principle of Democratic Centralism. The concerns have managers or works directors who are appointed by the superior state bodies, whose plans and directives they have to carry out and to whom they are responsible. In order to carry out the economic and social aims prescribed in the plans the managers have an extensive right of direction: they must guarantee not only the economic productivity of the concern, but also its good political and social development and they must be a model to all the workers within it.

The two principles of management and of collaboration by the workers ought, theoretically, to complement each other. However, the terms of the statute book already show a clear precedence between them. It is quite apparent that the emphasis lies on the central direction at the expense of the democratic, collaborating element. Furthermore the workers generally do not use their rights of collaboration directly, but by means of trade union representation in the concerns. Of these the statute says that they 'organize the creative collaboration of all workers in the working out and fulfilment of plans, in managing the

concern and in educating them to a high degree of social awareness'.[3] The trade union administrators represent the interests of
all workers in a concern but they are elected only by the trade
union members in the concern and require confirmation by the
superior trade union bodies, whose directives they have to follow.

Besides trade union administration there are further institutions
for the collaboration of the workers: production committees,
standing advisory bodies, institutions for 'socialist competition'
and for 'innovations'. All of these, however, deal less with
decision-making than with advising on and carrying out the
directives of the central bodies. Their main task is to stimulate
productivity, facilitate measures for rationalization and to mo-
tivate the workers to greater efficiency, greater solidarity and a
collective attitude to work. To this end there are 'economic
levers' such as prizes, productivity-related earnings and honours
in the shape of awards and honorary titles such as 'hero of work'
which are more likely to meet an individualistic need for competition or achievement, rather than to support the principle
of collective work and the new social distinctions of earnings
and prestige.

These anti-egalitarian tendencies, compelled by economic
demands, are counteracted in the GDR by emphasizing the
social significance of work. This is done most effectively by
making the concerns the focal point of all social life. In many
respects the social and cultural organizations in the East German
concerns are indeed exemplary: clubs, libraries, cultural centres
and other organizations for further education in the concern,
the administration of workers' housing associations and social
insurance, discount shopping at the place of work, opportunities
for holiday travel and children's holiday camps—all these organizations make the concern a place where the worker does not
simply work and receive his wage but where he enjoys many
social privileges and opportunities. Membership of a concern
therefore plays a much greater part in the life of the GDR than
in the case of comparable workers in western industrial states.

Whether all this achieves the new quality of work and of living
amongst socialist workers which is sought by the ruling party,
must be seriously called in question. Admittedly the East German
workers like to make use of the social and cultural opportunities
offered to them, but they largely ignore the political strings

attached to these social services. The production councils and socio-political discussions degenerate into dutiful routine, to be got through without any great intellectual or emotional involvement. In many cases the worker feels part of his concern not because he is part-owner of it, but because its social surroundings affect his everyday life.

From all that has been said, an answer gradually emerges to the question posed in the heading to this section: for many workers, the formula of a 'rule of the working classes' is a proclamation from above but not a social reality. It is true that Marxist theory sees the nationalization of the means of production as the essential condition for the self-government and self-determination of the workers; however, the mere exchange of legal titles of ownership and the conversion from private capitalist to public property is not sufficient to make nationalization a positive and concrete experience for the individual worker. Public ownership is virtually the same as state ownership. The simple declaration of 'socialist ownership of the means of production' does not guarantee that workers in fact move from a dominated to a dominating role and thus become true masters of the political and social order. For the great mass of workers, the GDR is less a workers' state than a working state. Hard work, order, discipline, ingenuity and a desire for achievement—all these good German qualities also take pride of place in the everyday life of the GDR. The slogan 'what the people's hands have created remains the people's property' is a hollow-sounding formula which has no foundation in reality. Most workers in the GDR do not have the feeling, suggested to them by political ideology, that their contribution to public property helps to create and to increase their own possessions. In the GDR as elsewhere the 'rule of the working classes' is really the rule of an *élite*. Its focal point is the intelligentsia.

3 ÉLITE AND INTELLIGENTSIA IN THE SOCIALIST STATE

When the communists took over the eastern zone of occupation after the defeat of Fascism, they were able to count on the support of only a small minority amongst the population. The intelligentsia were even less ready to give support and loyalty to the new system than the average citizen. For the socialist system to assert itself in Germany it was therefore all the more important to appoint politically reliable persons to the political, economic and social key positions. After 1945 the Soviet occupying power and the German communists were concerned first of all to take over the leading positions in politics and administration. By a consistent process of de-Nazification, all those who had in any way supported the Fascist rule of the Third Reich were removed from office. In contrast to the western zones, the conquest of Fascism in the Soviet zone of occupation did not simply restrict itself to a principally ideological dispute with the past: in addition to fundamental changes in ownership it also included the radical replacement of personnel in political and administrative key positions. A new leadership which in the post-war years distinguished itself more by its political than its specialist qualifications, took the place of the former supporters and followers of the Fascist system.

The leaders of the new state were mainly recruited from the old guard of communists—those who had already shown their obedience to the doctrine of communism and its international headquarters in Moscow at the time of the Weimar Republic. For these communists the building up of the GDR meant the long awaited fulfilment of their dream of a workers' state on German soil. They considered it their main task to establish this socialist state firmly against all resistance from within and hostility from without. Therefore, during the first phase of the GDR in which the new system had to be created step by step under difficult conditions, political reliability and unanimity were vital to the formation of an East German *élite* and the question of specialist qualifications necessarily had to take second place.

It is, however, impossible for any state or social system to do without the co-operation of highly-qualified specialists from the intelligentsia for any length of time. After the collapse of Fascism and in consequence of the war, economic and social life could only be set going again with the help of sections of the 'old intelligentsia'. The new proletariat *élite* attempted to convince the old intelligentsia of the advantages of the socialist system. Since this had only a limited success, efforts were made to bind the intelligentsia to the new state by means of top salaries and social privileges. After 1952 particularly distinguished specialists in the fields of science and technology received salaries of up to 15 000 marks per month, about 30 times (!) that of the average monthly income of a worker.

The policy towards the academic intelligentsia was ambiguous. In the administrative, legal and teaching professions account was taken of political reliability from the start and a temporary decline in performance was accepted. In those professions which were important for economic or technological development, on the other hand, continuity was considered essential and material incentives were openly employed. Thus engineers, architects and doctors were for a long time able to ignore the political and social demands of the system and yet stand at the head of the incomes table for the GDR. In the view of the high rate of emigration of these particular groups, this was a virtual necessity. After the frontier had been closed, and more particularly, after a new 'working class *élite*' had been trained, it was no longer so essential to show such consideration for the 'old intelligentsia'. The aim of the SED was to create a new intelligentsia combining both political and specialist qualifications, being an integral part of the working classes and recruited chiefly from the ranks of industrial and agricultural workers.

There were two sides to this task. Firstly a large number of highly qualified staff had to be trained for all branches of economic and social life. The execution of this aim fell to the new educational system which is to be discussed in the next chapter. On the other hand it was clearly in the interests of the East German political *élite* to raise its own specialist qualifications. With the progressive development of the GDR as a socialist state, it became increasingly important for its leadership to be able to use the latest findings of scientific and technological research for the various state, social and economic tasks of leadership and administration. It was now possible for the formerly dominant political qualification to recede in favour of the specialist one, because the political reliability of officials had become more and more a matter of course with the consolidation of the political system.

'Cadre politics', as the selection and promotion of functionaries in the apparatus of party and state is called in socialist states, has for a long time now not depended simply on party discipline, nor can the correct outlook replace a lack of specialist qualifications. This 'specialization' of party work is evident both in the training of the leading cadres and, more generally, in the composition of the party as a whole. According to a report by the Central Committee at the 8th Party Conference in 1971, 95·3% of the members of party secretariats have had a university or vocational education. If further possibilities of 'cadre qualifications' at party academies and by correspondence courses are included, one can almost speak of an academic influence on political careers within the SED.

This change in the social and qualificational structure of the party and the fact that the new intelligentsia has attained a central importance in East German society has given rise to many interpretations and speculations regarding the élitist structure of this society. The question arises whether there has not come into being a new *élite*, which is not only distinguished by its specialist qualifications but which differs from the rest of the population because of them. Do not the holders of leading positions in state and party form a 'new class' (Djilas) which lays claim to supreme power and is recruited mainly from its own ranks? Is not East Germany, too, fostering a reign of technocrats who see themselves as the executors and administrators of economic and industrial decisions?

The supposition that a new political class has taken control in East Germany is founded on the fact that a relatively closed group has taken over leading positions not only in politics but also in the economic and social system. However, a closed *élite* in the sense of a new class would presuppose that its members were recruited largely from its own ranks and would differ visibly from the rest of the population in their social career patterns. Despite several pointers in this direction this is not so in the GDR. Its political, social and economic *élite* is not a closed ruling caste, but rather a variously structured, mobile academic *élite*, by no means free of conflict, which was able to become an integral part of society on the solid basis of its achievements.

Although the scientific and technological *élite* of the GDR has acquired a character of its own, it has not succeeded in replacing the political *élite*. Both groups are concerned not so much with excluding the other as with co-operation. This is certainly not free from conflicts, but in contrast with former times the divergences between the more politically and ideologically orientated group and the more pragmatic and economically orientated one are no longer fundamental political conflicts but deal with differences of attitude, breadth of experience, and social models whilst having basically the same aims.

Today the GDR possesses a broadly based and differentiated intelligentsia below the actual wielders of power, such as is found in every industrial society. After the years of austerity, East German society is gradually acquiring the traits of moderate affluence. This would be unobjectionable if the whole population had a share in enjoying these developments, for an improvement in the general standard of living is, after all, one of the original aims of socialism, in contrast to many of the ascetic manifestations of its early years. The door to general affluence is wide open to all East German citizens in the shape of social and welfare organizations, educational opportunities and cultural facilities yet they already appear to take all these for granted. It is, rather, the great range of private spending and, in particular, the plight of pensioners living just above the poverty line, which strikes a discordant note. The latest socio-political measures on spending taken by the East German leadership, are therefore directed especially at these underprivileged groups. The fact that they became necessary shows that even in a society based on achievement and welfare as in the GDR its advantages and its drawbacks are very closely linked, despite all proclamations of a new socialist morality and community.

4 WOMEN AND THE FAMILY

The position of women in the GDR shows to what extent the idea of achievement has become a generally valid maxim in East German society, both as a right, leading to social advancement, and as a public virtue arising from a universal duty. Women's rights and duties in the GDR are largely identical with those extensive rights and duties which apply to every active citizen of the state. In the GDR, equality does not therefore simply mean equal treatment in the formal legal sense, but equal opportunities in a society based on achievement.

From the standpoint of women's equality, the GDR can point to a proud record in nearly all spheres of public life: of the 500 representatives elected to the People's Chamber on 14 November 1971, 159 were women, about four times the number of women

members in the West German parliament. Women are also found
in numerous other leading positions in social and political life.
From the outset, equality of opportunity was not only a constitutional principle but also a social one. This is true especially
of professional life. In the GDR the employment of women has
always played an important part, going far beyond that of comparable industrial states. In recent years it has risen constantly,
reaching 48·7% of all employed persons in 1971; in the case of
workers and employees it even exceeded the number of male
employees with a total of 50·2%.[4] Today three-quarters of all
women and girls of working age are actively employed in the
GDR. All in all there emerges the picture of an almost total
integration of women in the labour force. In the GDR, women
represent the same reserve force of workers for which the Federal
Republic depends on its immigrants.

It would, however, be superficial to see women's employment
in the GDR as simply remedying a deficiency. It is, at the same
time, a fundamental socio-political requirement derived from
the principle of equality. In the view of Marxist theorists, from
Marx and Engels to August Bebels and further to Clara Zetkin,
women will only have equality of opportunity when they also
have economic equality with men. In the socialist system, equality
between men and women implies their equality in a working
capacity.

This idea of the emancipation of women reflects the socialist
image of man, which sees the true fulfilment of the 'socialist
personality' in work and traces all cultural and social phenomena
back to the conditions of work. Emancipation is regarded not
only as a liberation from traditional, paternalistic dependence
but rather as an acceptance of the general duties of a citizen. In
the GDR the citizen is above all a worker, regardless of sex.

Now even socialism cannot ignore the biological fact that
women play a part in human reproduction which cannot be
identical with that of the opposite sex. A state such as the GDR
whose economic productivity is endangered by its age structure
must, in particular, seek to improve its birth rate. The involvement
of women in the work process on the one hand and the population
policy on the other are thus two aims which must lead to conflicts
both for the social policies of the state and for the women themselves. The state is attempting to resolve this dilemma by various

measures designed to increase the birth rate and to help mothers—ranging from direct prizes for child-bearing to promoting part-time work for women. Although East German organizations are exemplary in this respect, women are still overstrained as a result of this dual role. When faced with the alternative of a career or motherhood, women appear to opt for the former, as the growth in female employment and the further decrease in the birth-rate show. The more liberal attitude to abortion therefore has serious consequences as regards a population policy, and attempts are being made to counteract them by increased incentives for child-bearing.

With all this emphasis on the emancipation of women in their working capacity, the GDR has never wished to give up the institution of the family either ideologically or in practice. On the contrary, it has been allotted a central role in socialist society and in the new Code of Family Law of 20 December 1965 it is described as 'the smallest unit of society'. This makes it plain that the aim of socialist policies regarding the family is not to uphold the scorned bourgeois concept of the family as an intimate private grouping but rather to involve it directly in the socialist system. The state leaves the family its function especially in the field of education, whilst giving it a clear social objective. The code of family law (*Familiengesetzbuch*) of 1965 is the clearest expression of this programme for the socialization of the family.

There are two ways in which this socialization is to take place: the family acts on behalf of society and, at the same time, hands over to society part of its traditional functions. This may be seen both pragmatically and ideologically. On the one hand a family where both parents are working—this is true of almost a third of all mothers in the GDR—can no longer perform the variety of tasks in the fields of child-care and education which formerly fell to the family. On the other hand, society is now taking over family functions in the public sphere in order to subordinate them the more definitely to the socialist educational system. Today places are available for more than half of all children under 6 years in crèches, kindergartens and weekly homes for children; indeed, the GDR has created a system of pre-school education which can well serve as a model, both didactically and in organization, for similar efforts in other—even western—countries. Where there are still insufficient places, neighbours and pensioners in particular are expected to help to look after the children of mothers at work.

This demand for joint help and action is the focal point of all educational and propagandist efforts on the part of the state to bring about a new socialist morality. From reading the relevant manifestos, the GDR could almost appear like a new 'extended family'. All aspects of life, including family life should be part of a general social life and be closely linked with it; conversely general social life for its part should take on a few quasi-family traits. All citizens of the GDR are regarded as belonging to a large blood-brotherhood, pledged to build a new social order. Any individual not recognizing this task and duty should be brought to an understanding of it by means of social education rather than by state coercion. Thus the everyday atmosphere of the GDR, as reflected in its press and in the relationship between those in power and the population, reveals a very strange mixture of Utopian visions of the future and traditional paternalism. The intention is that one great state family should grow up from a society of equal workers under the eyes of benevolent state elders.

The politicization of society and the socialization of private life have, admittedly, not been as successful as one might be led to think from official self-portrayals. They have, if anything, produced a counter-reaction resulting in a greater withdrawal into the family. While society plays a larger part in politics, the family plays a correspondingly smaller one: here people want to follow their own inclinations and wishes, free from the constant pressures of achievement and morality.

It would, however, be a biased viewpoint to see the great prominence given by the East German people to the family as a refuge for private life simply as a withdrawal from the total demands of socialist society. It is in this very region of private and family life that general tendencies of an industrial society, German social traditions and the socialist structuring of society strangely coincide. The diminution of a broad family relationship to a small family unit, its disappearing function as an all-embracing institution, the surrender of its economic and cultural concerns to society as a whole and, at the same time, the greater privacy and intimacy given to marriage and the family are tendencies which we can observe in all industrial societies. Because of this, any strict allocation of roles to men and women, where men are restricted to the sphere of production and earning outside the home and women to their domestic capacity within it becomes increasingly anachronistic.

A new understanding of equal rights and partnership must necessarily give women greater scope in their careers where they can realize their full potential without thereby calling in question such institutions as marriage and the family. Yet in the GDR too this movement towards emancipation comes up against tenacious social traditions, which are also observed and deplored there. As regards the public sector and institutions, conditions have largely been created for women to achieve equality of opportunity, but the actual realization of this is counteracted by prejudices, such as the fixing of allegedly typical careers and positions for men. Even now women's work still has the character of substitute help or of tasks considered necessary but which men—secretly— would not wish to do. The extent to which this gulf between official pronouncement and actual facts still exists even in East Germany is seen in the fact that, while the qualificational structure for career women has largely approached that of men, most intermediate and top positions in the economy, society and the state are still predominantly held by men.

The picture of the emancipation of women and their equal rights is therefore not as rosy in the GDR as might appear from its own ideological interpretations. Here too, as in many other spheres, it can be seen that it is easier to transform the institutional framework than traditional values of society. East German women will only achieve true equality of opportunity when their share of professional and social positions is no longer merely the result of staffing shortages or a proportion dictated from above, but is the natural expression of the will of society as a whole. As long as the socialist leadership emphasizes the duties rather than the freedoms of the new order, there will be much that remains artificial and that will be undermined in everyday life. Despite all efforts by the GDR to create a picture of women and families corresponding to the conditions of our industrial world and of social justice, Karl Marx's dictum is still a valid touchstone even in East Germany: 'Social development can be measured exactly by the social standing of the fair sex (the ugly ones included)'.

5 GIANT ORGANIZATIONS

The socialist order as regards government and society proceeds from the unity of state and society and the identity of private, social and state interests. According to the claims of this all-embracing ideology there can be neither any private sphere set apart from the public one, nor any aspect of society that is autonomous or even independent of politics. In the socialist system of the GDR, therefore, all social organizations are simultaneously political and state organizations and serve the policies of state and party.

With its system of social organizations (or 'giant organizations' as they are called in the GDR) the political leadership is attempting to get the whole of society into the grip of its organizational power, to link up with the specific attitudes, interests and activities of its various groups and sections and to make use of these to further the expansion of its social policies. The social organizations are therefore not the product of free social enterprise from below but the result of a planned structuring of society from above. It is therefore not surprising that the giant organizations are closely linked both in structure and staffing with the political leadership and especially with the state party, the SED. They are the social executive organs of state and political authorities, whose guidelines and basic decrees they transform into practice. Lenin's description of the giant organizations as 'transmission belts' gives a vivid picture of their function.

The educational and propagandist work of the giant organizations, which are also called 'schools of socialism', can only be successful if they are not merely concerned with conveying and carrying out orders but rather with converting these into forms appropriate to the various social groups. The mass organizations must therefore not simply be regarded, as under earlier ideas of totalitarianism, as instruments used by the ruling SED. They are at the same time organizations to further the interests of their members. They must also take *their* interests and affairs into account if they wish to be successful as rulers. To this extent the flow of communication is by no means one-way—towards the giant organizations—for information is also conveyed from below—that is, from the members to the political leadership.

Despite the well-developed apparatus of party and state, the giant organizations are not easily dispensable, nor could they be absorbed by the others. Were they to be abolished, the party would be in danger of being overtaxed in its organization of society and also of becoming an enclosed ruling caste, receiving no information whatever from society. Especially if the aim of effective unity in socialist social policies is to be achieved, it is important that the giant organizations should not be identical with the party but should retain their own character beside and below the party.

A glance at the individual giant organizations shows how the functions of party instrument and membership interests are combined in this seemingly contradictory manner. The largest of them is the Free German Association of Trade Unions with a membership of over 7·2 million employees. This is the vast majority of the (approximately) 8·3 million employees in the GDR; if one takes into account the fact that members of co-operatives are not allowed to join this union, firms in the GDR can be regarded as 'closed shops'. Almost every worker or employee is a member of a union.

In the socialist system of the GDR the unions do not represent the interests of employees against employers since, according to the ideology of public property, employers are, of course, the employees themselves. From this standpoint it becomes clear why there can be no right to strike in the GDR and why collaboration in increasing productivity is the main task of the unions. They act as intermediaries between the central planning authorities and help in putting state decisions and directives into practice in the individual concerns. The unions and the union management in the concerns organize socialist competition so that it becomes an extensive mobilization of the workers for achieving ever higher output. This continual spurring on gave the unions the reputation amongst workers, during the first decades of East German history, that they were more concerned with exploiting them than with representing their interests. It is noteworthy that it was the behaviour of the unions which substantially contributed to the revolt of East German workers on 17 June 1953, which, as is well known, began with a protest against the raising of production quotas.

The leadership of the GDR and the Federation of Trade

Unions have learnt their lesson from these events. It is true that increased productivity, now as then, is one of the main aims of the trade unions, but employees are no longer treated as passive objects but are actively involved in the production process. The unions take care to see that targets are not simply presented to the concerns but are discussed with them and are effected in such a way as to take into account and even encourage the physical and spiritual capabilities of the workers. The unions organize and control industrial safety and professional qualifications and they help to provide a wide range of welfare services including holidays. In 1971 almost 90 000 places were available in the holiday homes run by the Federation and over 1·1 million holiday trips were organized by it.[5] The Federation is also entirely responsible for the administration of social security. These many advantages of membership ensure that union membership becomes a matter of course for almost every East German worker or employee.

The Free German Youth organization can be seen as a kind of young people's trade union. It exists to integrate young people into the evolutionary process of socialism and also offers a multitude of opportunities in the most varied fields. Today this organization has almost 1·7 million members, while its pioneer organization 'Ernst Thälmann' (called after the communist leader in the Weimar Republic) has a membership of over 1·8 million children between the ages of 5 and 14. Thus about 65% of all young people between the ages of 14 and 25 are members of an organization, but their membership figures vary considerably: whereas approximately 80% of students, high-school pupils and young soldiers are members of Free German Youth, the corresponding figure for young industrial workers is around 50% and in the case of young agricultural workers falls to 20%. These figures make it clear to what extent membership of Free German Youth is necessary for professional and social progress in the GDR.

Young people are regarded as 'pacemakers for socialism', they are systematically involved in the rights and duties which apply to every adult in the GDR. They are also represented in almost all state and political bodies, up to and including the People's Chamber where they have their own party with 40 members through the monopoly of their association, the Free German Youth.

This carries out its task of educating the children and youth of today to be the socialist workers of tomorrow, by providing a wide range of activities. Today's young people have an individual, moderately critical character of their own and are critically loyal to their state.

During the last few years the giant organizations have lost some of their character as monolithic instruments of party power and have become more concerned with their group functions. Thus they no longer serve to propagate a totalitarian and rigid view of all sections of society but have become a structural element of a society which is aware of differing interests and social groups, even in the official attitude of its leaders. These interests are taken up by the organizations and conveyed to the political leadership, which is supposed to take account of them and include them in the general interests of socialist society. Admittedly this does not yet mean that a pluralist, free society in the bourgeois, western sense has taken the place of a totalitarian society, but the scope of social activity has increased—and with state approval. It can be said that the giant organizations are developing from being subdivisions of the political system into relatively autonomous bodies which give a social service.

6 THE CHURCH ON THE FRINGE OF SOCIETY

In socialist policies for society, no place has been left for the Christian churches. The fate of the churches in the GDR can be seen as the successive displacement of religious institutions to the fringes of society. It is the aim of socialist policies to fuse public and private spheres together as much as possible. Such a policy cannot allow any institutions other than those sanctioned by the state to perform social functions. For this reason it is the parties and giant organizations which increasingly carry out tasks which formerly fell to the family and non-state social organizations including the churches. Since, in materialistic philosophy, the Christian churches can have no part or only a subsidiary one in fulfilling the socio-political tasks of the socialist state, they were systematically deprived of all but their directly *ecclesiastical* social functions and restricted to a purely religious sphere. Under the pressure of the state, the churches in the GDR have had to revert back to being simply institutions for worship, no longer having general social tasks such as kindergartens, schools or hospitals. Because of this, the churches have lost their institutional support in society. Where religion has become a purely private matter with no influence in public life, the church can only be regarded as the focal point of social life in a purely geographical sense.

Despite these tendencies, over two-thirds of the population of the GDR are still members of religious communities. The great majority of nominal Christians in East Germany belong to the Protestant Church (approximately 13 millions), about $1\frac{1}{2}$ millions are Catholics. This unequal distribution also explains why the conflicts between the SED and the churches took place principally with the Protestants. The policy of the SED towards the churches had two main aims: firstly, it strove to push the church to the fringes of society and to restrict church life purely to holding services; secondly, the churches which until recently had still been linked with those in West Germany were to decrease their politically undesirable bridging function and finally to give it up altogether. The main cause of more resolute action on the part of the SED against the churches—whose attitude towards the SED during the 1950s had been one of rejection and reservations —was the so-called Military Agreement on Religious Welfare of 1958. This was between the West German churches—still linked with those in East Germany by means of common institutions— and the Federal Government to ensure the provision of religious care for the army. The Protestant church leaders in the GDR thereupon felt obliged to agree to a declaration of loyalty towards the SED régime, in accordance with which Christians, like other citizens, had to fulfil their civic duties on the basis of socialist principles. The bishops declared that, as Christians, they respected the development towards socialism and wished to make their contribution to the peaceful construction of the new state. In return, the GDR leadership renewed the guarantee of religious freedom, which has remained embodied in the Constitution of 1968. Ulbricht himself declared in the People's Chamber in 1960 that Christianity and the humanist aims of socialism were not opposites.

The arguments between church and state in the GDR received great publicity in the West until well into the 1960s, because they seemed particularly suitable for attacking the lack of freedom in East Germany. It is impossible to speak of a specific battle against the churches or even of a ruthless persecution, yet there has undoubtedly been a systematic repression of church influence on public life. One example of the long-standing conflict between church and state was the state-run *Jugendweihe* (Dedication of youth), a secular substitute for confirmation, following Marxist philosophy. This example shows the attempts made by the party to deprive the churches of their traditional social functions and to replace the religious church cult by a party cult inspired by its philosophy (this was also done with marriages, baptisms and funerals). The churches came off badly in this conflict and were finally forced to give in in the interests of their members. Whereas Protestant clergy formerly declared that *Jugendweihe* and confirmation were incompatible, they are now prepared to confirm even those children who, chiefly on account of their social and career prospects, had decided in favour of *Jugendweihe*.

The outcome of this struggle points to the fact that the church in the GDR is gradually retreating and has had to relax its opposition to the régime. Under the pressure of political conditions it has had to learn that it may no longer take its bearings from traditional ideas of the past, with its close ties between church and state, and it has learnt by experience that it would do better to follow its own difficult path than to follow its 'brothers in the West'. Meanwhile most of the Protestant and Catholic church leaders in the GDR have realized that the most advantageous way of fulfilling their church tasks is to make peace with the state. They accept the authority of the socialist state. Only recently Bishop Schönherr, the chairman of the Confederation of Protestant Churches in the GDR declared: 'The church will oppose all attempts to militate against the state.'

The consequence of this difficult and painful lesson was the loosening of ties between the Protestant churches of East and West Germany and the establishment at the beginning of the 1970s of a 'Federation of Protestant Churches in the GDR', completely independent of the church organization of West Germany. Thus, after many years of scepticism and inner resistance, the Protestant church has at last found its way to a critical solidarity with the socialist state. Because of this policy, the church is in the position today of practising and maintaining its religious and, where possible, social function, within the limited framework granted to it by the socialist régime and its social policies.

The Catholic church, too, has learnt to come to terms with the political conditions and has both sought and found a kind of pragmatic agreement with the new state. Such agreement between the churches and the socialist state certainly does not imply that they have given up or watered down their Christian beliefs in favour of a Marxist philosophy. It simply means that they have given up opposing the state and disputing its legitimacy. The most probable advantage of this policy is that they will be able to pursue their religious tasks more thoroughly and undisturbed and will, in future, not have to expend energy on constant conflicts with the state.

For this reason the real danger facing the churches in the GDR today is no longer a direct confrontation with the state, but rather a progressive shrinking and inner atrophy. This is not only the consequence of the active socialist social policies, it is also the result of secular energies and tendencies, liberated by the progressive process of industrialization, which contribute to a lessening of traditional religious bonds everywhere. In the everyday life of the parishes, the shrinking of the churches is already in full swing, not least as a side-effect of the growing prosperity of East German society. Numerous parishes have already dwindled down to a small handful of worshippers, if that. But since the church in the GDR—unlike that in the West—does not have the opportunity of compensating for its dwindling religious substance and attractiveness by social activities, it is hit all the harder by the process of secularization. It is this, together with socialist policies, which is threatening to turn the church into an institution on the fringes of society.

1. cf. Storbeck, Dietrich, *Soziale Strukturen in Mitteldeutschland* (Berlin 1964), 14 ff.
2. GBA, section 2, para. 4.
3. GBA, section 12, para. 1.
4. *Statistisches Taschenbuch der DDR 1972*, 32.
5. ibid., 512.

7 | The educational system

In our industrial age, education and training, knowledge and research possess great importance for the economic, social and political development of all countries regardless of their governmental and social systems. The growth of national economies depends increasingly upon the extent to which new scientific and technological knowledge is gained and how quickly it can be applied to the productive process. In the GDR too this universal phenomenon known as the 'scientific and technological revolution' has become a key concept for understanding society and a central factor in both political propaganda and the state activities of planning and management.

Science and technology are not only important and decisive factors in economic development, they are also both cause and effect of radical changes in the structure of society. In modern industrial societies there exists a social mobility, determined primarily by the educational system. Professional and economic prospects or the social rise and fall of an individual depend more than ever before on his qualifications obtained through that system. Educational opportunities and their realization in the various societies have become not only the driving force behind social development but also the criterion for judging the social position of the individual. In the industrial age, the educational system has thus become the most important condition for the economic, social and democratic achievement of every state.

In the GDR, educational policies have always been regarded as social policies and must be understood as such. The changes in the educational system of the GDR therefore reflect the general political and social history of this state and are an essential part of its development. This is already seen in the basic laws on education which the GDR has passed during the quarter century of its brief existence. The 'Act concerning the democratization of schools' came into force as early as 12 June 1946 during the Soviet era and applied to all *Länder* then occupied by Soviet forces. It brought about radical changes in staffing and organization throughout the educational system, parallel to the economic and political reforms already mentioned: expropriation, land reform and de-Nazification. Corresponding to the programme of the first phase in the GDR, this act extended to anti-Fascist measures (purging and recruitment of teaching staff) and to democratic reforms (introduction of a general 8-year education for all). It was superseded by the Act of 2 December 1959 which encouraged the 'socialist development of the educational system in the GDR' and which laid down, in particular, that polytechnic education should be a central part of the socialist system. This Act expressed the ideas of 'transition to socialism' characterizing this era, just as in the later phase of 'developing socialism' which began in 1963 the 'Act concerning the uniform socialist educational system of the GDR' of 25 February 1965 became the legislative basis for the further development of the whole educational system. This Act of 1965 was incorporated in the new Constitution of 1968, especially in clauses 17 and 25, and put into effect in numerous decrees and decisions regarding schools and universities, vocational training and adult courses. The primary aim of the whole educational system of the GDR, according to the preamble to this Act, is the creation of an 'educated nation'.

The title of the Act of 1965 states the underlying principle of the educational system: its uniformity. This is true of its organization, planning and execution. It is characterized by its grouping of all educational institutions—from nursery schools, general polytechnic high schools, vocational and adult training centres, universities and specialized institutes right up to such cultural institutions as libraries and cultural centres—into one system of interlinked educational establishments. Forging these links between the various institutions with regard to their pedagogic aims, teaching courses and opportunities for transferring from one to another is the task of a central administrative body. Only a few months after the capitulation of the Nazi government, a *Deutsche Zentralverwaltung für Volksbildung* (Central German Administration for People's Education) was established in the

Soviet zone of occupation in July 1945 with the aim of guaranteeing uniformity in educational policies, despite the rivalries between
the still existing *Länder* in cultural and educational matters. In
the GDR today there is no sign of that federal organization of
the educational system which is so characteristic of West Germany: in East Germany all educational institutions are subject
to the planning and management of the central state bodies,
according to the principle of democratic centralism.[1]

The organizational uniformity of the educational system is
intended to guarantee the uniformity of its teaching courses and
aims. The content of these courses combines intellectual and
scientific training with moral and social education, the theoretical
dissemination of knowledge with practical work experience, and
general with special education. Teaching is centred on scientific
and sociological subjects and stresses the close relationship
between the two groups. In both cases it is the understanding
of the 'inherent laws' which is stressed, since this is a central
category in Marxist theory and pedagogy. Science teaching is
based on the laws of the scientific and technological revolution,
while sociological subjects deal with the laws of the Socialist
revolution: the official attitude is that both revolutions are
not simply inter-related but rather that they are, in essence,
identical.

The uniformity of the GDR's approach to education is based
on a uniform view of man. It is the Marxist-Leninist view which
seeks to penetrate all political, social, public and private areas of
society. This idea of a 'new man' is the guiding principle behind
the all-embracing task of education; it does not restrict itself
only to the educational institutions themselves but pervades
school training at all stages, the cultural activities of the giant
organizations and all mass media. The whole of the GDR is
regarded as an all-embracing 'educational society': all social
and all pedagogical institutions and relationships are to throw
light on each other and work more closely together. It is indeed
the will of the political and ideological leadership that the society
of the GDR should be one vast school, a school for education in
socialism and for producing the 'socialist personality'.

The 'new man', that fundamental concept in the Marxist
scheme of education and society, is, above all, a working individual. He is to find his true existence and self-realization in

work, but in work which has a totally new quality when compared to work conditions under capitalism. Manual and intellectual work, administrative and executive activities are to grow ever closer together and finally fuse. The ultimate goal of a communist society is a society of highly qualified workers. Although it is officially admitted that this goal is not yet in sight, all present-day measures are supposed to be directed towards it. In the case of the socialist educational system this means that it should aim at a growing standard of education for *all* workers, not at producing highly qualified technologists and scientists who differ from the broad mass of workers in qualifications, cultural awareness and way of life.

In Marxist theory, work as a means of self-realization pre-supposes not only a general rise in the standard of qualifications but also demands new attitudes which see work as a form of social productivity. Individual efforts in work or achievement should be discouraged and be absorbed within a collective work morality. Socialist education in the GDR must therefore be regarded not only as a general and vocational training corresponding to the latest academic findings but also as an education in socialist behaviour especially as regards work. Education and training for work as a social activity are therefore the focal point of courses in all educational establishments, not simply in those specializing in vocational training. Thus section 5, paragraph 3 of the Education Act of 1965 requires of all school pupils, apprentices and students that they should be educated to have 'love and respect for work and for working people. They should be prepared to do manual and intellectual work, to participate in the life of society, to take responsibility and to prove themselves in work and in life.' In the GDR, pedagogy implies education leading to the socialist person, knowledge implies collaborating in the development of socialist technology, society and the economy. Both education and knowledge therefore have an instrumental function in the GDR; they must translate into reality those standards and aims which are required of it by socialist society—in practice, the working classes—and its leading party, the SED.

E

2 THE SCHOOL SYSTEM

The focal point of the East German school system is the comprehensive school. The traditional division of the German school system—after a common 4-year primary schooling—into *Hauptschule* (secondary school) giving a general education, *Realschule* (technical school) offering courses leading to commercial and technical careers and *Gymnasium* (grammar school) preparing pupils for entry to university was already abolished during the early era of Soviet occupation in the 1946 'Act concerning the democratization of schools'. Its place was taken by a common and compulsory 8-year elementary school, which was changed during the 1950s into a compulsory 10-year high school. Today the 10-form general Polytechnic High School is the 'basic type of school in the uniform socialist educational system'.[2]

The introduction and development of the Polytechnic High School was seen in the GDR as a deliberate step towards changing society. It was intended to overthrow the traditional system of 'class schools'. The comprehensive school was regarded as a deliberate uprooting of the bourgeois educational privilege, as a democratization of the educational system to bring about a true as well as a formal equality of educational opportunity for all children. In this respect the Polytechnic High Schools of the GDR can really be called 'people's schools'. They are the clearest manifestation of the socialist aim of a general rise in educational standards.

The adjectives 'general' and 'polytechnic' describe the central educational content of the 10-form High School. They are used to convey the socialist idea of man as an individual, realizing his potential through work in society. In the educational system of the GDR, then, general education must be understood to mean polytechnic education.

Thus polytechnic instruction is seen as the introduction to the socialist process of work. It is a subject of general education transmitting a basic technological, economic and social training and intended also to have a bearing on all other subjects.

In all school subjects the choice of teaching material should be determined by the working world: thus, for instance, the reading matter in German lessons and the arithmetical examples in mathematics should be taken from the everyday life of a state-owned industry. This is known as the polytechnic principle. In addition, there is a specific school subject dealing with polytechnic matters. Here, during their last years in the upper school, the pupils learn the basic skills of industrial careers, they are introduced to technical drawing, the organization of a socialist concern and to working life in general. For a time, this 'polytechnic instruction' was simply a sort of apprenticeship for upper-school pupils, a predetermined training for a career. Today it is a fixed component of general school education. In this way the GDR has succeeded in relating all forms of education firmly to the working and professional world—in strong contrast to the traditional German educational system. To anyone with an idealistic or classical concept of education such a development must appear suspect. However, the interest of western educationalists in this subject and the basic principles underlying it shows that the GDR has made an original and exemplary contribution to educational practice and research in industrial states, which is of importance to both socialist and bourgeois systems.

Admittedly polytechnic education can never be a socially and politically neutral general education on a technological and industrial basis, but is closely bound up with education for 'conscious socialist citizenship with active participation in the life of society'.[3]

Social and political education in the GDR does not simply deal with social and political connections, it deals, above all, with the socialist doctrine on behaviour and morality. It is intended to introduce children to the socialist virtues and especially the virtue of work from an early age. In this region of socialist education the schools are supposed to work in close collaboration with parents and especially with the youth organizations, the Free German Youth, and its children's organization the Ernst Thälmann pioneers[4] (section 7 of the Education Act of 1965). According to the uniform and comprehensive view of man in Marxist and Leninist theory, there should be no division between the public and private sphere or between the areas of home, school and out-of-school. All must obey the command to educate the 'new man'.

In this respect the educational and school system of the GDR is total in the sense of all-embracing. Whether it can also be described as 'totalitarian' depends not so much on its range as on its educational aims. Are they really directed towards the self-realization of every individual and are they determined by each individual for himself? The categorical way in which the leading party expresses the aims of socialist education, the assurance with which it takes for granted the identity of individual and social interests, together with the impression that this education for work is education for collective achievement rather than a self-fulfilling activity—all these suggest that the GDR is concerned more with teaching affirmatory attitudes and behaviour than with explaining political and economic connections within various systems including its own.

The general 10-form Polytechnic High School is the particular institution within the educational system of the GDR in which the democratic claim of training all-round, educated personalities is seen most clearly. Being a comprehensive school it aims at influence in breadth and seeks to avoid training an *élite*. However during the past few years developments have been observed which contradict this socio-political maxim and result in a differentiation within the school system.

For principally economic reasons, the GDR cannot do without such a differentiation which takes account of individual talents and capabilities, if it wishes to make use of an intelligentsia to deal with the tasks arising out of the 'scientific and technological revolution'. The demands of economic and industrial progress and social development may, in the official ideological view, be identical; however the question of 'Uniformity and Differentiation in the educational system' (the title of a publication by the Academy of Educational Studies, Berlin 1971) shows that in practice the two ideas may become separate and contradict each other. The leadership of the GDR is continually trying to balance these two elements, economic-technological and socio-democratic development, and to bring them into line with its ideological beliefs, but the outcome of these efforts remains ambiguous. The example of the socio-politically necessary uniformity of the school system on the one hand and the economically justified differentiation on the other shows once again that the GDR is neither a socialist state, set apart from general industrial developments, nor an industrial state estranged from socialism. In reality the state is more complex and more precariously balanced than socialist ideologists in the East or followers of the theory of convergence in the West would like to have us believe.

3 UNIVERSITIES AND HIGHER STUDIES

In every modern industrial society, a university education is the most important qualification for obtaining a leading position in the state, in economics, society or culture. Clearly, therefore, it was one of the first concerns of socialist policies to change the staffing of universities and to shift the balance from a preponderance of staff and students with a bourgeois background in favour of those from working-class homes. The first of the three university reforms in the GDR took place between 1945 and 1949 and concentrated on this problem of personnel. When the universities in the Soviet zone reopened for the winter semester of 1945–6, it had been decreed that the 'bourgeois privilege of education' was to cease. For specially talented and politically reliable children of industrial workers or agricultural labourers, special pre-university institutions were established; these were later incorporated into the universities as 'industrial and agricultural workers' faculties' and led to degree courses. Not only such preparatory courses but, more directly, the actual favouring of working-class children was meant to compensate for the former preponderance of those from middle-class homes in higher education. Whilst the 10-form High School is intended for all children—90% already attend it—the 2-form Further High School leads on to university entrance. In schools leading on to higher education at least 50% of the children were now to come from working-class homes and they were also to be given preference in obtaining university places. Until well into the 1950s, the consequence of taking social background into account was that many highly qualified middle-class children had to take second place to less able working-class children. This was one reason for the large number of refugees particularly amongst young people.

This policy of a deliberate anti-privilege campaign could be abandoned at the beginning of the 1960s when the social composition of the student body had become approximately equal to the social structure of the total population and it became important for the economic development of the GDR to make use of all its educated people—including its bourgeois reserves. Today obtaining a place in higher education once again depends primarily on individual achievement: preference on social grounds is only given in cases where a particular subject attracts more suitable candidates than there are places. Working-class students now receive help more indirectly by means of preferential treatment in the extensive system of scholarships and student allowances which benefit over 90% of students in the GDR.

The second goal of this initial attempt to reform the universities was to bring about a change in the teaching staff. After the collapse of Fascism, the Soviet occupying power and the German communists were concerned first of all to remove all National Socialists amongst the teaching staff from their posts and to retain a sufficient number of those who were bourgeois and 'anti-Fascist' to get the work of the universities going again. Only after a politically reliable 'new intelligentsia' with specialist qualifications had been trained was it possible to make increased socio-political demands on the 'old intelligentsia' and to replace them.

The transformation of universities in the GDR into socialist universities was the object of the second university reform during the years after 1951. This was not so much concerned with staffing as with the content of courses and research. Following the Soviet model, university study was subjected to strict regimentation, an academic year of ten months was introduced together with a system of graded stages and intermediate tests. Today, university courses in the GDR consist of a one- to two-year course of basic study, vocational training lasting, as a rule, two years (a qualification for practising a career), one year of specialist study leading to a diploma examination and, finally, research. The basic studies obligatory for all courses reflect the socialist concept of general education: it should convey scientific, sociological and vocational knowledge; in addition all students are expected to improve their knowledge of Russian, and take part in sports and national defence activities.

In all universities in the GDR, Marxism and Leninism occupy a central position in both teaching and research and special institutes have been established for these studies, such as the Institute for Sociological Studies (run by the Central Committee), the Karl Marx Party High School or the 'Walter Ulbricht' Academy for Political and Legal Studies in Babelsberg. This last is a training-ground for leading positions in the state and the law and especially for young people seeking a diplomatic career in the GDR.

However, it is not only sociologically-orientated institutions which are required to concern themselves with Marxism and Leninism—these philosophies are to pervade all academic disciplines. In the view of the guardians of Marxist and Leninist doctrines within the apparatus of party and education, these doctrines are not simply important in all branches of knowledge, they are fundamental. They are regarded as the primary study, the very basis of all political, sociological and intellectual effort. This totalitarian conception of knowledge is incompatible with a bourgeois view which proceeds from the autonomy of each subject, the plurality of its methods and the statement of its own problems. Yet in the academic life of the GDR, the conflicts and pressures were not limited solely to argument with the bourgeois academic attitude and its final exclusion; they revolved above all, around the question as to what the true teachings of Marxism and Leninism really were and who should be entrusted with the task of establishing this 'truth'. During the 1950s, at a time when the dogmatic attitudes of the SED leadership were hardening, numerous academics who saw themselves as Marxists and Leninists, were accused of 'revisionism'—for example, the philosophical schools of Ernst Bloch and Georg Lucaĉs, the proposals for reform put forward by the economists Behrens, Benary and Kohlmey, and the economic and social historian Kuczynski. In 1956 Wolfgang Harich, a pupil of Bloch, attempted to transfer the Polish 'thaw' to the GDR, an attempt rewarded by a lengthy term of imprisonment, Less than ten years later the physicist Robert Havemann had to learn the hard way how serious it is to question the supremacy of the required interpretation of Marxist and Leninist social teachings, as laid down by the party leadership: after calling for a critical examination of these dogmas, he was removed both from his teaching post and from his place in the Academy of Sciences.

All in all, however, the party leadership did allow universities and higher studies a looser rein during the 1960s. The relationship between politics and academic studies changed from the previous clear subordination of the latter to one of equal, though unstable, co-operation. The reasons for this change were, on the one hand, that the SED leadership now felt more sure of the political and social reliability of its academics, while on the other hand their studies were expected to contribute to greater dynamism in economic processes and growth. The new tasks of laying the foundations of a planned new economic system by means of scientifically based prognoses on technical, economic and social trends could only be achieved by introducing new methods such as operational research, cybernetics and systems theory. Together with the economic reforms after 1963, several previously despised subjects such as empirical sociology took on a new lease of life.

After the plethora of new academic disciplines and new beginnings in research during the last few years of the Ulbricht era—when 'system' became the very key-word in dealing with all phenomena and their explanation—the party leadership has, since Erich Honecker took over the office of First Secretary, once again given everything the clear stamp of Marxist-Leninist philosophy. Thus the new development with its tendency towards a more 'objective' approach by means of 'de-ideologising' has come to a halt. It is not the fact that Marxist-Leninist philosophy is given a central role in the economic system of the GDR but the way in which it is upheld and reiterated which creates that academic atmosphere appearing so sterile from a western viewpoint because it uses so many words to say so little and apparently always the same. It is not Marxism and Leninism as such but the monopolistic party attitude to its interpretation and the application of its teachings which makes the reading and analysis of academic publications from the GDR a frequently tedious, indeed exhausting task to an outsider.

The progressive interweaving of academic theory and economic and industrial practice, of university studies and business life is the object of the third university reform which was begun in 1966 and is to be completed by 1975. It is above all a reform of structure and organization. A university is directed by a rector, a council, one academic and one social committee. The number of these gives the impression of a fully-fledged co-operative, but this is misleading. Even the organization of universities and their subordinate bodies is subject to the principle of 'democratic centralism', with individual direction and individual responsibility and the merely advisory function of the collective bodies. The council is composed of representatives of various university groups and advises on questions relating to studies and general university development; the academic committee decides the research programme of the university and has authority to confer degrees and appoint teachers; the social committee is concerned with the socio-political tasks of the university and staffing policy. The membership of both committees includes, in addition to university teachers, student representatives and those appointed by firms co-operating with the university.

If 'democratization' was the main principle of the first university reform and the creation of a 'socialist university' the chief aim of the second, the focal point of the third reform is streamlining. It aims to give a particular orientation to the individual universities within the economic production process and its academic and technological preparatory work. Thus the individual universities specialize in different areas of research which correspond to the economic structure of their geographical location. The University of Jena, for instance, where the third reform was introduced, has been concentrating on research into toolmaking in conjunction with the Zeiss works there. A large part of research undertaken by East German universities—over 80%—is commissioned by industry. Co-operation agreements are concluded between the firm and the relevant university section setting out the aim and the financing of these research projects. In the long term it is envisaged that industrial concerns and university sections will be amalgamated into large-scale research associations.

The universities and their research have been brought into the direct service of technological and economic development. They are to guarantee the 'test-runs' for scientific innovations which are essential to technological and economic progress in an industrial age. For the development of the university as a place of universal research and study, this has the danger of every subject being assessed by its short-term contribution to economic productivity. In such a development it is academic teaching which suffers because it takes second place to research as do basic research and problems which overlap different subjects.

4 PROFESSIONAL AND ADULT EDUCATION

The GDR has created a system of professional and adult qualifications which is a firm part of the educational and economic system as a whole. The extent to which these qualifications are linked with changing economic requirements is seen, for example, in the number of correspondence courses run by high schools and technical schools. The lack of qualified personnel, evident in the social structure of the GDR and further intensified by emigration in the 1950s, meant that it was undesirable for a large number of workers to be away from the production process because they were studying full-time. Many of those who left high-school with leaving-certificates were able to obtain their university qualifications by means of correspondence courses running parallel to vocational training. Today a quarter of all students registered at East German universities are external students and in the case of technical students their numbers rise to as high as 40%. The advantages of this arrangement are obvious: pressure on the universities is relieved, academic study and the active practice of a career can influence each other and the external students remain part of the production process. In contrast to these social advantages, the disadvantages principally affect the individual student; the double role can strain psychological and physical endurance to the utmost. Attempts are being made to lessen this danger by a well-tried didactic method of combining external and full-time study and by paid leave from work.

The Code of Work of 12 April 1961 (paras 61–6) requires all works managers to devise schemes leading to qualifications and to use these as a basis for entering into contracts of qualification with the individual workers. These qualifications can be obtained within the concern in question as well as outside it, in 'works academies' (*Betriebsakademien*) or in people's high schools (*Volkshochschulen*).

Much of the work of adult education has, in the GDR, been assigned to works and businesses. The 'works academies' offer many opportunities for further qualifications ranging from specialist vocational training to university degrees and professional diplomas. During the last few years, one out of every four workers in industry obtained further qualifications whilst employed at one of the 1200 'works academies' or 1000 rural village academies. In 1966 29% of university graduates, 46% of specialist diploma students and 40% of technical workers completed their training within the framework of adult education.[4]

This extensive system of achieving qualifications near to one's place of work is, of course, only possible in an economic system which aims at concentrating centres of work into large-scale concerns and where the individual concern is subordinate to the authority of state and social organizations. In this way the planning of a system of education and qualifications can become an integral part of general economic planning. As so frequently happens, it has become bogged down in bureaucratic regulations, yet even here attempts have been made for several years to put the planning on a long-term and more scientific basis. Pedagogic research in particular has, in recent years, broken away from its shadowy existence amongst Marxist and Leninist sociological studies and has taken over modern sociological methods of field work and educational prognoses.

One example of the collaboration of economic planning and pedagogical research is the change in the system of professional training since 1967. Most training schemes for apprentices are reduced to a new set of basic occupations which take account not only of the current state of professional qualification requirements but also anticipate future development. For these basic occupations in growing branches of industry new training schemes are being worked out which will be valid throughout the economy and which aim at a synthesis of general and specialist knowledge, including both theoretical and practical training and extending from elementary to advanced courses.

This ambitious concept of vocational training directed more towards the industrial occupations of the future than to traditional mechanical jobs and crafts can only be achieved with great financial and organizational efforts. Here too the GDR is breaking new ground by seeking to overcome the traditional 'dual system' in German vocational training—the separation of theoretical education in the vocational school and practical training at the place of work—by establishing 'works vocational schools' (*Betriebsberufsschulen*). Today almost half of all those learning vocational subjects receive the whole of their vocational training at their place of work.

Thus in the GDR the place of work has become a focal point not only in economic and social life but also in the educational system as a whole. It opens up innumerable opportunities for its workers which, however, also increase their dependence on it.

The overlapping of rights and duties, fundamental to socialist ideology and teaching, is particularly apparent in the educational system: those to whom the state gives the right to be educated have the social duty to make use of this right. Applied specifically to vocational training this means: 'All young people have the right and the duty to learn a trade or study for a career.'[5]

5 THE SOCIALIST MERITOCRACY AND EDUCATION

If we analyse the various organizations in the socialist educational system of the GDR to consider their capacity for achievement from an economic, a social or a democratic standpoint, our judgement is most positive from that of economic progress and organizational efficiency. It is true that the educational system, being part of a centrally planned and guided economic and social system, is not unaffected by the bureaucratic excrescences and insufficiencies of such a system, but it is characterized by a high degree of synchronization between the individual institutions promoting education, which could rarely if ever be attained in the federal system of West Germany as regards cultural matters. The GDR has created a uniform system of education, offering wide opportunities of transfer and new beginnings within and between a great variety of institutions. Without a doubt this system contributed more than any other factor towards making the GDR an 'efficient, modern industrial state' as the preamble to the Education Act of 1965 puts it.

The close interweaving of economic planning, forecasting labour requirements and guidance in the choice of both subject of study and future career ensures not only that there will be staff to fill all types of posts as necessary but makes it possible to offer each student, during his last year of study, a firm appointment after the successful completion of his course. To a bourgeois liberal observer this may seem to lead to a restriction of opportunities for education and development in individual cases, yet objectively speaking, it must be admitted that no one in the GDR is forced to embark on any particular course of study or career, and that entry to certain of these is restricted solely because there are already too many people in them. Thereby the basic right of freedom in the choice of career is certainly limited but, at the same time, the state also restricts the problematical freedom to choose a training which might possibly lead to unemployment or social downgrading. The channelling of all training by the state should therefore not be considered only from the standpoint of a total economic increase in productivity, because for the individual it has a not unimportant element of social security. In a planned system he can assess and organize his career prospects far better than in a capitalist society where, after all, the vagaries of the market decide the success or failure of all he has invested in his education and training.

Taken as a whole the GDR satisfies the demands made on its educational system by economic and technological developments so well as to put it almost at the head of other comparable industrial states. Yet an examination of the social and democratic aspect intended by the régime leads to a rather less positive judgement. By means of its educational system the GDR has certainly become a highly mobile society in which education and achievement are the principal factors affecting social mobility upwards or downwards. Whether the democratization of the educational system and its qualifications really lead to the realization of the official programme, which aims to unify the private and working life of all workers, must be strongly doubted. Many reports and impressions of daily life in the GDR seem to suggest that the chances for social mobility upwards and downwards have become more equal for everyone, but not working habits or ways of life. Horst Siebert attributes the fact that East German society has not become a 'classless society' but rather a 'well-differentiated meritocracy' primarily to the educational system.[6]

The 'new man', the 'all-round, educated socialist personality', that ideal of social and educational policy in the GDR is more of an ideological façade than social reality. According to official pronouncements it is not highly-qualified technocrats but highly-trained socialists with specialist qualifications and socialistically-minded specialists which the educational system is intended to produce. Yet what Marxist-Leninist social theory and its exponents in the GDR proclaim to be a fusion of a new quality between human capabilities and human behaviour which has already been largely achieved, is often only an apparent fusion to which lip-service is paid under the pressure of socio-political propaganda. Anyone who wants to be anyone in the GDR, who wants to grasp the innumerable educational and career opportunities must profess himself to be a faithful socialist. Thus many display social and political attitudes which in fact they do not possess.

However contradictory it may sound, the fact that socialist awareness is not more widespread than it is, is due to the actuality of socialist education in the GDR. As long as this education in the political sphere consists mainly of pronouncements of 'laws' from above instead of explaining the political and social conditions, as long as it aims, in the sphere of work, to increase productivity and boost morale instead of ensuring the self-determination of each worker, socialism will not, it is true, be unfamiliar to a large section of the population, but neither will it be a philosophy which has been entrusted to them and which they have made truly their own.

Thus the educational system of the GDR may be seen as having two sides to it, just like so many other social spheres of this society. It opens up opportunities for its citizens which indisputably belong to the essentials of a democratic society but it links these with forms of education which do not emancipate but rather require affirmation and produce a one-sided attitude. Professional openness and social mobility such as are guaranteed by the educational system to a large extent, have no corresponding intellectual mobility and political openness which ought to be the aims of any educational system that claims to be democratic.

1. cf. paras 69–76 of the Education Act of 1965.
2. Section 13 of the Education Act of 1965.
3. ibid., para. 2.
4. Siebert, Horst, *Bildungspraxis in Deutschland* (Düsseldorf 1970), 149.
5. Section 25 paragraph 4 of the Constitution of 1968.
6. Siebert, op. cit., 154.

8 | The economic system

The economic structure of the GDR was affected far more by the division of Germany than was that of the Federal Republic. Until the end of the war, the economy of eastern Germany had been closely linked with the rest of the country and there were considerable differences within it as regards development and industrialization. Whereas Mecklenburg and Pomerania were primarily agricultural, Saxony and Thuringia as well as the area around Berlin were very highly industrialized. Overall the proportion of those employed in industry in 1939 was actually greater in eastern than in western Germany (57% to 48%), but industry in the East sent almost two-thirds of its products to the rest of Germany or abroad, while conversely it obtained over half its industrial goods from other regions of Germany, thus underlining the close links between them.

The economic separation of this region both from the former eastern German territories and, more especially, from West Germany thus brought a host of new problems to the country's economy. The GDR not only had to solve the problem of an unbalanced economic structure; but in addition the severing of its economic ties with West Germany (which during the course of centuries had developed organically) presented enormous difficulties. West Germany, by contrast, was far better able to compensate for the economic consequences of separation because of its connections with other western countries. The structural weaknesses of the newly independent East German economy are most obvious in the road and rail network: whereas in the former Reich the most important arteries ran from west to east, the present GDR needs to concentrate most on those running from north to south. All the major waterways whether Elbe or Oder end either in West Germany or Poland and even the canal system meets the needs of the GDR only to a limited extent.

The structural disadvantages of the East German economy, caused by the division of Germany into two states whose economic systems hardly even communicate with each other, were further worsened by the policy of reparations, pursued by the Soviet Union during the first few years after the war. Admittedly the economy of East Germany was affected no more badly by the war than West Germany, but the Soviet demands for reparations weakened the East German economy to a degree greatly surpassing those losses suffered by West Germany through industrial dismantling. All in all, the effects of the war and the dismantling of industry reduced the economic potential of the GDR by almost half of what it had been before the war (45 %).

It is hard to ascertain the amount of reparations provided by the eastern zone. The Russians had demanded ten thousand million dollars and it is assumed that they received that amount. Western estimates put it at 40–60 thousand million marks (10–15 thousand million dollars), and even the SED in 1965 spoke of reparation payments in the region of 25 thousand million marks. Whilst the West German economy received a strengthening shot in the arm from 1948 onwards by means of the Marshall Plan which, together with the currency reform was the start of the 'economic miracle', the economy of the eastern zone was not allowed to accept the American offer of help nor could it count on any comparable aid from the Soviet Union. Quite the reverse; the GDR was subjected until into the 1960s to a price discrimination policy by its main trading partner, the Soviet Union, and generally had to pay back all credits obtained from the Soviet Union punctually and with interest.

Adverse structural conditions as a result of division, excessive demands for reparation and the absence of generous economic support thus characterize the unfavourable starting point of the East German economy after 1945. Judged by such a start, what has been achieved in the meantime is more than remarkable. The GDR is now amongst the ten largest industrial nations of the world, its standard of living, though still noticeably below that of the Federal Republic, is by far the highest throughout the whole of the eastern bloc and the annual gross national product of the GDR has increased fivefold between 1949 and 1969. It is therefore not surprising that the expression 'economic miracle', once coined to describe the phenomenal rebirth of the West

German economy, is now being applied with some pride by the GDR to itself. It is even convinced that with the far less favourable beginnings of its economy compared with that of West Germany, its own achievement is even greater than the West German 'economic miracle'. Nor is it very surprising that in its economic successes the leadership of the GDR sees an endorsement of the socialist economic system which it has built up.

The difficult conditions facing the reconstruction of the GDR economy were worsened at the outset by the political demands of transforming an inherited economic system into a centrally administered one. It is true that in 1945 the Soviet Union by no means insisted on the total abolition of a capitalist economic structure in its zone and its immediate transformation into a socialist economy, but its development did proceed step by step towards a socialist system on Soviet lines. Elements of the capitalist system did not have to disappear everywhere and not completely, but they were so weakened and so strictly regulated that they could no longer have any decisive function within the economic system. This acceptance of the Soviet model brought additional difficulties to the economy of the GDR. The expropriation of estates and of industry together with the expulsion of landowners and industrialists brought about a temporary lack of qualified managers. The problem of insufficient qualifications also arose in setting up the managerial offices necessary to a planned economy and for many years these were staffed by many functionaries who had not received adequate training for their posts. Finally—and this is of particular importance—the massive scale of emigration to West Germany, especially through the loophole of West Berlin, contributed towards a considerable drop in both the number and quality of the potential work force in the GDR. Between 1952 and 1961 when the Wall was built, no less than 2 200 000 citizens of the GDR fled to the West; of these about two-thirds were in active employment and amongst these refugees the number of certain highly qualified groups was above average. Using the numbers of refugees, which were always particularly high during years of economic difficulties, it can be proved that the motives of those fleeing to West Germany from the GDR were not only political but in many cases also economic. The massive emigration to West Germany only became an increasing economic problem during the 1950s: in the first few years after the war there was still an excess of workers. The strength and incalculability of the flow of refugees made the planning of the economy even more than normally difficult and undoubtedly harmed the production capacity of the GDR. Since the building of the Berlin Wall, therefore, the economy has been freed of one of its worst 'disturbance-factors'. For these reasons the building of the Wall, inhuman as it may seem from the standpoint of liberty and freedom of movement, is regarded with good reason as an important step in the consolidation, growth and qualitative improvement of the GDR economy.

2 STAGES IN ECONOMIC POLICY

During the time of their occupation (1945–9) the Russians, in agreement with the German communists, aimed at changing the socio-economic structure. It was to this end that the agrarian and industrial reforms were carried out, thereby inhibiting any development of private or capitalist forms of production within that zone. The next stage was the construction of a centrally planned economy, begun in 1947 and based on the Soviet model, and this, despite a number of internal reorganizations, has characterized the economic system of the GDR until today.

Both aims—the ever progressing socialization of the means of production right up to the total 'victory of socialist production conditions', as well as the constant improvement of the planned economy—have moulded the development of the economy during the last 25 years. Of course the active pursuance of these aims threw up a number of problems of greater or lesser difficulty, which forced the leadership to adapt the general direction of their economic policies to particular conditions arising from the political and economic situation. There can, however, be no doubt that the economic and political aims of the SED throughout were the perfecting of the central economic steering mechanism together with ever increasing socialization. Thus transformed, the inner structure of the East German economy was not only made to conform to that of the Soviet Union and the other countries of the eastern bloc, but in its external relationships too it was incorporated firmly into the socialist economic system dominated by the Soviet Union. Futhermore, in its economic policies, the GDR has largely adopted the aims and methods of the Soviet Union. Only now as a result of its economic successes has the GDR reached the position where it can follow national economic policies which serve its own interests, though admittedly without wishing to risk any serious conflict of interests with the Soviet Union.

The development of the East German economy took place in the following individual stages. The first stage from 1945 to 1949 was aimed at rebuilding the economy whilst at the same time changing the bases of power by means of agrarian and industrial reforms. The SED calls this stage the 'conquest of political and economic commando heights' by means of which the balance shifted in favour of socialist ownership of the means of production together with the removal of power from all privately owned parts of the economy. After the establishment of the GDR in 1949, this process of socialization was purposefully continued. This second phase, continuing into 1962, strove to develop socialist forms of production: this is the phase of transition from capitalism to a developed socialist system. By the end of 1962 this phase of transition is regarded as having been completed. From that time onwards one speaks of the 'victory of socialist production conditions' in the GDR. Only from this time onwards, so it is said, could the economic laws of socialism come to full fruition in the GDR.

Economically and politically the most recent, socialist phase (1962–7) was first of all determined by a reorganization of the economic system, calling itself the 'New Economic System'. This was superseded in 1967 by 'the economic system of socialism', although there are no fundamental innovations in this classification. The 'new' economic system is, briefly, an attempt to remove the inefficiencies of a centrally planned and steered economy by giving a greater share of responsibility to individual concerns. The present phase (since 1967) is determined by this complicated attempt to harmonize the demands of a state-controlled economy which are regarded as indispensable, with individual responsibility given to concerns and producers. In party-political terms this is described as helping the economic laws of socialism to reach their full development whilst guaranteeing firm political control of the economic process.

If one considers the development of the East German economy without paying too much attention to ideological explanations, the following picture emerges. After the enormous difficulties at the beginning, already mentioned, the GDR concentrated during the 1950s on counteracting the structural weaknesses of its economy by a planned rebuilding and extension of its industrial installations and by the development of basic industries such as the electrical, chemical and engineering industries in particular. This was intended to correct the worst effects of dismantling and the structural 'disproportions' in the economy. This aim has been achieved to a certain extent, though admittedly at the cost of satisfying the consumer interests of its citizens.

During this stage the plan for the economy is that instrument of governmental control which ignores all those elements that normally regulate the market. The plan is drawn up by a state commission, approved by the political authorities and carved out with the help of an extensive executive apparatus. During the course of its history the GDR has made many experiments with such plans. There have been two 5-year plans, and one 7-year plan as well as all the annual plans. Today there is, in addition to a long-term plan of, usually, 5 years, the annual plan which is in fact, if not formally, identical with the state budget. The long-term plan of perspective which, in contrast with former plans, is supposed to be based on searching economic prognoses, is the effective steering instrument of East German economic policies, but has more scope for flexibility than former long-term plans.

The centrally planned system, taken over from the Soviet economy, which governed the economic process of the GDR up to the development of the New Economic System introduced in 1963, was built up on the following principles:

1. Economic production levels were based on figures pre-determined by the central authorities.

2. Prices, likewise, were fixed by the central authorities over considerable periods of time.

3. Individual production units were obliged to produce those quantities decreed for them and if possible to exceed them.

4. All external economic activities were controlled by the state

and adapted in particular to the economic system of the eastern bloc, controlled by the Soviet Union.

By means of this planned economy, the GDR was able to achieve some of its aims (the restructuring of the economy, the building up of new fields of production, and increase in productivity and economic integration with the eastern bloc) but at the same time it had also to accept serious defects in the economic system especially by comparison with the economic policies of western countries, in particular the Federal Republic, which are based on a free market economy. The main defects of a centrally planned economy were that the real needs of the economy were frequently overlooked; that the plans themselves were not flexible enough to be adapted to new situations and that the carrying out of each plan took pride of place without regard for either real needs or the quality of the products, instead of being based on principles of economic viability.

The GDR succeeded in achieving above-average annual rates of growth (between 5 and 10%, the highest increases being in 1958 and 1959). This, however, led the political leadership at the end of the 1950s to attempt to increase the output of the economy still further with an ambitious 7-year plan. The aim of this was not only to reach but even to surpass the living standard of the West Germans. The sensational failure of this 7-year plan whose high expectations could not even remotely be fulfilled, plunged the GDR into an economic crisis, or rather a recession and lessening of growth rate at the beginning of the 1960s, which could only be overcome, finally, by the introduction of the New Economic System. Only then could there be a renewed and constant upward trend in the economy with an average annual growth-rate of 4·5% during the 1960s.

3 THE NEW ECONOMIC SYSTEM

Because of the period of weakness in its economy during the 1960s, the GDR leadership came to realize that the old methods of planning and the organization of economic processes were no longer adequate for the demands of a highly-developed industrial economy. The ambitious 7-year plan was dropped and replaced by short-term annual plans, supplemented by others with a longer perspective. The result of this process of rethinking was the New Economic System of Planning and Management, officially propounded and introduced by Ulbricht in 1963.

It is true that the leadership of the SED would hardly have ventured on so radical a reorganization of its economy had not the Soviet Union also felt a need for reorganizing its own planned economy. The first theoretical exponent of the new economic policy was the Soviet economist Libermann. Following the discussion arising from his theories, the GDR transformed its economic system even more extensively than the Soviet Union. In the eastern bloc the GDR has become almost a model country for the new type of reformed non-liberalized planned economy.

The essence of the New Economic System is that the central state planning machinery is restricted to the formulation of long-term economic aims (perspective plans), allowing individual firms a greater responsibility, governed by principles of viability and efficiency. In concrete terms, the GDR economy had to improve the relationship between supply and demand, build up the most productive branches of its economy and promote re-search into and development of those branches of technology most important for future growth. Furthermore, economic efficiency was to be increased by greater flexibility and adapt-ability in planning, by the introduction of the cost-benefit principle instead of thinking solely in quantities, and by better insight into all stages of the economic cycle in order to obtain more reliable information for the various decisions to be made. The idea of a planned economy was certainly not given up, but rather directed towards the so-called perspective (flexible aims), whereas the economic system was supposed to function within this framework by a 'closed system of economic levers'. In short, the New Eco-nomic System meant a departure from the old planning practices and it contained certain concessions to the principles of a market economy which, however, did not go far enough to allow a 'self-regulating economy'. At first, planning on the one hand and a self-regulating economic process on the other were more or less evenly balanced.

The carrying out of this reform proved to be extraordinarily lengthy and difficult. First of all the completely obsolete price system had to be reformed so that the true cost of a product and the capacity of a concern could be better calculated. To this end price reforms were needed on three occasions. Moreover the actual value of individual industrial installations had to be established anew to obtain a basis for working out profitability. Finally, new forms of management and co-operation with state departments had to be developed to ensure the greatest possible economic effect. In the course of this development it was, above all, the guiding control of the state that underwent change.

4 THE MANAGEMENT OF THE ECONOMY

In the constitution of the GDR the management of the economy has been called the main task of the Council of Ministers. To carry out this task, it makes use of a broadly based apparatus of different institutions. In the front line of these is the State Planning Commission which has been called the 'economic general staff' of the Council of Ministers. The duty of this commission is to translate into concrete terms the individual economic policy decisions taken by the Council of Ministers influenced by the Socialist Unity Party in the background. The Planning Commission is responsible for drawing up the long-term plan as well as for the individual annual plans. The last long-term plan covers the years between 1970–5 but even in the middle of 1972 it had not yet been definitely settled. The annual plans must in each case be adjusted by the Planning Commission so as to follow the aims of the long-term plans.

The drawing up of a plan is a complicated process in which many institutions, right down to individual concerns, participate. The State Planning Commission has the overall task of laying down the individual spheres of planning for the various industrial ministries. The ministries must translate the tasks allotted to them into concrete requirements and pass them on to the Association of State Co-operatives subordinate to them, while these in turn share out the detailed execution of the directives amongst the individual co-operatives. The Association of State Co-operatives is a combine of a large number of concerns in one particular branch of industry, e.g. the pharmaceutical industry, whose task it is to plan, direct and co-ordinate all production within a particular sphere and to see that it is economically viable. At their head are the general directors, the economic bosses of the GDR. During the drawing-up stage of the plan the state co-operatives themselves carry out the important duty of allocating the various tasks in detail to the individual units of production. On the basis of these results the concerns then work out their own annual plan of production and make the necessary arrangements with their suppliers and their market outlets etc. in order to enter into such contracts as shall ensure the concrete realization of the tasks set by the plan.

Once the plan has reached this stage, it follows the same course back to the Planning Commission and the Council of Ministers which finally approves it and puts it before the People's Chamber to be enacted. Amendments are possible at all stages. The end result is an obligatory economic plan, generally for one year, specifying exact tasks for individual concerns. Naturally the various tasks laid down by the Planning Commission are not decided arbitrarily but are based on preliminary work by both the planning commissions of the individual concerns and of the associations which possess their own long-term planning departments. Moreover the Central Planning Commission is supported by a Ministry of Science and Technology whose research council is responsible for forecasting scientific and technological developments. The Planning Commission also runs its own Economic Research Institute as well as an advisory board for economic research in which problems of planning are scientifically worked out and the results incorporated in the plan during its formation.

Parallel to this centralized structure of production there is also some regional organization. About three-quarters of industrial production is centrally controlled, the rest being run by 'regionally controlled industry' by means of regional economic councils. These, together with the regional planning commissions, look after the planning and execution of such infra-structural measures as are necessary for the fulfilment of the plan. The regions are also the competent authority on such questions as the siting of industries and the availability of staff and services for the centrally controlled concerns.

Within the industrial structure of the GDR the combine is playing an increasing part. A combine includes larger industrial units as for instance the Leuna chemical works at Merseburg under one single management whereas the Association of State Co-operatives has been formed from individual state-owned concerns which remain independent. Large combines are directly subordinate to a ministry, others belong to one of the Associations or are governed by a regional economic council.

The basic unit of the socialist economy is the socialist industrial unit, *Volkseigner Betrieb* (VEB). These are individual factories or service organizations of varying size which produce goods or provide services and are, collectively, the property of socialist society. The various production units work on the basis of the state plan and are obliged to apply the economic laws of socialism and to increase public socialist property. This means increasing productivity, ensuring economic viability and harmonizing the social and personal interests of the employees. Every concern receives one capital grant and a current fund from the state as laid down by the central plan, and with these it has to operate economically; in addition it receives financial payments for awarding prizes to its workers. In return it must contribute specified dues to the state.

Every nationalized enterprise has a director at its head, appointed by the state according to the principle of democratic centralism. The director is personally responsible for the management of the enterprise, but is also obliged to work in close cooperation with the Communist Party organization and with the trade union. These can, however, only make recommendations, not give directives.

The salaries of the managers are fixed by the government and differ according to the size and capacity of the enterprise. In many cases they are several times as much as the average working wage. Within each enterprise there is a grading of incomes based on the principle of efficiency. In this way each individual can improve his income by greater output and by gaining additional qualifications. This has proved to be an effective stimulus to the work process.

The wages for different types of work are fixed by the state in conjunction with the trade unions on the basis of work quotas. Strikes as a means of enforcing wage demands are not possible in the GDR since it is assumed that a state ruled by the working class can do nothing which is against the interests of the workers.

The New Economic System of 1963 gave a key position to the Association of State Co-operatives and invested their directors with a large share of responsibility for the efficiency of their production capacity. However, during the course of carrying out the reforms, the state authorities considered it advisable to diminish once again the autonomy granted to the general directors of the Associations and to the managers of the concerns. Since 1967, certain tendencies pointing to a return to the old type of a centrally administered economy have become unmistakable. Moreover, the legal position of the Associations and their relationship to their member concerns has not been sufficiently clarified. In the unanimous opinion of competent observers, the aims which the reform of the economic system hoped to achieve have only partially been realized. The reform came to a halt after 1967 and failed to make effective, in particular, the proclaimed 'closed system of economic levers' which was meant to include such factors as wages dependent on performance, prices, costs, profits, interest and credits. Nevertheless the economy of the GDR appears in a far more favourable light today than during the 1950s, when an all too rigid control by the state suppressed all spontaneity and individual responsibility in its economic partners. In particular it has now succeeded in relating production more to its true cost and to quality, thereby achieving, overall, a more economic use of the means of production. Admittedly the GDR will not be in a position, for many years to come, to overtake the Federal Republic with regard to productivity and standard of living which was once its stated aim, for, in spite of all its successes, the difference in productivity between the Federal Republic and the GDR is at least 25% and is even estimated at 30% for the standard of living, However, this cannot diminish the fact that *within* a socialist economic system the GDR has undoubtedly been highly successful. The standard of living of the East Germans is the highest in the eastern bloc, and production methods in the GDR are more modern than in the countries of its socialist allies. It is indisputable that in the case of East Germany, German hard work and efficiency together with the ready-made traditions of a developed industrial country have fruitfully combined to achieve such good results in spite of permanent difficulties arising out of the mechanics of planning.

In 1971 the average income of workers and employees in the GDR was 800 marks per month (about £90–120). Improvements in income are fixed by the state in conjunction with the unions and, as a rule, depend on increased productivity and economic growth. In contrast to western industrial states, most households in the GDR spend almost half their income on food, whilst this item makes up only 35% of the family budget in the Federal Republic. On the other hand, rents, gas and electricity are extremely cheap, compared with western prices, making up only 6% of the average budget as against 20% in the Federal Republic. It is chiefly the lower income groups which profit from the cheapness of living accommodation, basic foodstuffs and transport, whereas better-class goods and luxury articles in particular are extremely expensive by western standards. Thus a far-reaching levelling of living standards amongst East Germans is achieved in practice.

Compared overall, both the economic strength of the GDR and the standard of living of its citizens fall well behind those of the Federal Republic; however the East Germans do live considerably better today than before the war, even if they are still well removed from the western type of affluent, consumer-orientated society. 'Compared with the pre-war period there are less people today who are exceptionally well-off, but there are also far fewer who are exceptionally badly off. There are both ideological and sociological reasons for this, but it does produce a feeling of economic justice and social security which are not found to the same extent in the Federal Republic.'[1]

Here we seem to have an important criterion for comparing the two systems which must be taken into account with any comparative statistical information. Indisputably the West German standard of living and its economic productivity are higher than those of the GDR. Nevertheless the benefits of increasing productivity of the East German economy and a constantly rising standard of living—despite a number of remaining shortcomings in the availability of consumer goods—are more evenly distributed amongst the people as a whole than can be said of the Federal Republic with its great disparities in income and wealth. It is not by chance that the present form of the capitalist system of West Germany is being increasingly criticized from within, because it has produced an imbalance between very unequally distributed private wealth and public poverty and because it is not able to satisfy the need for social justice and social security as the socialist system does. Social justice and security are, after all, fundamental human needs at least as much as the need for an ever higher standard of living.

For these reasons an economic system will not be judged exclusively by its perfomance in production and the optimum use of its capacity nor by its ability to satisfy individual needs—the yardstick of social justice and security must also be applied. If these criteria, which are so hard to incorporate in a purely statistical comparison, are included, the comparison between the two economic systems is not so disadvantageous to the GDR as statistical productivity values and conventional calculations regarding the standard of living would indicate. There is much to suggest that the majority of the East German population would prefer to see a combination of the relative advantages of both systems. The dilemma of this 'rivalry of systems' is the very fact that such a combination is impossible. A free choice by the East Germans of the system under which they would like to live is out of the question, politically speaking, for the foreseeable future.

5 THE ECONOMIC SYSTEM OF SOCIALISM IN THE LIGHT OF THE POLITICAL ECONOMY OF THE GDR

Historians of the GDR date 'the victory of socialist production conditions' back to 1962, but, of course, it is not really a question of a fixed date but rather of a gradual transition to the economic system of socialism.

What, then, is meant by the victory of socialist production conditions? The phrase means that 'socialist methods of production have finally established themselves in all spheres of the economy'.[2] Socialist production is that which is based on social ownership, as opposed to capitalist systems, where the means of production are privately owned. Indeed, the proportion of socialist concerns in the GDR has grown steadily, amounting to a little over 50% following the industrial and agrarian reforms in 1950 and rising to over 80% at the present time. All large and important industries are publicly owned, only smaller concerns, especially those specializing in crafts, still being run privately although they are subject to strict state control and heavier taxation. Approximately 10% of the gross national product of the GDR comes from semi-state concerns. These are a hybrid form where the private owner gives a (compulsory) share in his enterprise to the state which then exercises control over production and management. Without a doubt, therefore, the great majority of all concerns today is state- or, rather, publicly-owned. According to East German economic theory, the predominant socialization of the means of production is the indispensable precondition for the unrestricted effectiveness of the economic laws of socialism.

What are these frequently invoked laws of socialism? In this connection an economic law does not imply empirical legality in the sense of a natural law, but rather a norm, an obligation. Thus the 'motive force behind the socialist method of production', which is regarded as the basic economic law, is paraphrased in the following words: 'It demands the constant broadening, perfecting and intensifying of socialist production on the basis of the latest scientific and technological findings, to strengthen the socialist order and to effect a constant improvement in the material and cultural needs of the citizens, in the development of their individual personalities and their socialist social relationships.'[3]

In our opinion this basic law means no more and no less than an obligation to bring about a constant and qualitative improvement in the output of the economy using both science and technology as aids to further the interests of the socialist state and its citizens. In addition to this basic law there are also special economic laws as, for instance, the law of distribution according to merit (merit principle) and the law of planned, proportional development (growth principle). A further much discussed economic law of socialism is the law of the economy of time. Like all these laws it has a standardizing character. This law aims at 'a general strengthening of the socialist society by a constant saving of working-time, materials and money and a systematic improvement in the living and working conditions of the workers'. Just like the basic economic law, this law of the economy of time is very easy to understand. It simply states that the optimum result is to be achieved with the available economic means and within as short a time as possible. Allied to this law is the law of 'constant increase in productivity', such an increase being synonymous with the previous law where the time factor remains the same.

Thus the socialist laws are, in reality, appeals to all those involved in the production process to work and to produce more, better, more efficiently, more economically and more quickly etc. In fact, the basic economic law is only a kind of summary of the individual laws of socialist economics. Accordingly, too, it is always emphasized that the effectiveness of the individual laws can only be understood and practically applied in connection with the basic economic law. Admittedly East German economic theorists constantly repeat that the economic laws of socialism are not simply appeals to satisfy social needs but are themselves strict laws, for instance when they state that the economic laws are the 'inner necessities of economic life under given social conditions' or that the economic laws determine economic development. This is correct in so far as it is obviously important for the development of the economy and the satisfaction of social needs that productivity should be increased and that the quality of the products should be constantly improved, but these are commonplace matters to which the lofty title of 'economic law' should not be applied.

As regards the ideology of the system, however, the conception of economic laws serves it well. On the one hand it conveys the idea of a theoretical understanding of economic activity and on the other it is a useful method for explaining the difficult problems of the past and the tasks of the future. The economic problems of the past were that the economic laws of socialism could not be fully effective because different conditions of ownership prevailed and because western imperialism (not least on account of the open Berlin frontier) disturbed the development of the economic laws of socialism. For the future everything depends on ensuring full effectiveness for the operation of these laws. Since they are not laws in the academic sense of the word but can all, in the final analysis, be reduced to the idea of constant economic improvement, every practical economic activity can somehow be related to them: central planning, the work of the concerns and that of the individual. If therefore the results of economic development are not as good as expected, then the economic laws of socialism have not been sufficiently observed or have not been sufficiently understood and applied by the workers. If the results are good they are interpreted as manifesting the undisturbed development of the economic laws of socialism. Since, in actual fact, these laws are obvious and banal they can be expressed without difficulty in stimulating slogans which are all aimed at spurring people on to greater efforts.

Morally speaking, the economic motive force of socialism is, in any event, far superior to the economic laws of capitalism in the eyes of East German ideologists, for in socialist society the interests of the great majority become effective, as opposed to the capitalist love of profits which benefit only a few. If, therefore, it is possible to make the workers even more aware of their true interests, then the driving force behind the socialist economy must continue to grow so that 'the concordance of personal interests together with the interests of the concerns on the one hand and the interests of society as a whole on the other are effectively put into practice wherever work is done'.[4] But who decides on the interests of society as a whole? As everywhere else in the GDR it is the working classes and their Marxist-Leninist party.

6 SOCIALIST AGRICULTURE

Within the economic system of the GDR no other sphere has been subjected to such radical structural changes and social transformations as agriculture. The GDR undertook the formidable and still uncompleted task of 'building a modern, industrially organized and productive agricultural system on the basis of a socialist economic and agrarian policy'.[5] The task was formidable not least because—as Engels and Lenin had already recognized—conditions in country areas and the political opinions of the peasants worked against any radical change in the bases of the economy or the forms of production particularly strongly; difficulties also arose because in all modern industrial societies today the problem of agriculture is acute and because convincing, imitable models of an efficient agricultural system, fully integrated into the industrial one, are not to be found in any of the existing economic systems. Seen from the standpoint of the integration of agriculture with a modern industrial society, the development of agriculture in the GDR is a remarkable experiment, the success of which can be taken as a model for solving the problem of agriculture in comparable industrial societies. Already today the GDR has attained a leading position within the eastern bloc, as regards its productivity and organization.

Changes in the agricultural system of the GDR came about in various stages. Their basis was the abolition of the traditional structure of private ownership in favour of collective ownership of the means of production. By means of the agrarian reform of 1945, large estates of over 100 hectares were expropriated first and a relatively equal agrarian structure with innumerable small and medium-sized farms was created, still based mainly on private ownership. The collectivization of agriculture was begun in 1952 on a purely voluntary basis, with the formation of agricultural collectives, *Landwirtschaftliche Produktionsgenossenschaften* (LPG), and was completed in 1960 under massive pressure from the state. This aimed both at socializing the land and at creating larger and more efficient units. Today 86% of all agricultural acreage in the GDR belongs to the agricultural collectives, 7% to large state-owned estates of over 800 hectares, and the rest is distributed amongst agricultural concerns owned by public bodies, e.g. the churches, or a few isolated farms which cannot become part of a collective on account of their geographic position.

The leadership of the GDR gave its farmers a choice of three different types of collectives. Type 1 simply provides for the collective use of all arable land, while all other means of production remain in private hands. Type 2 provides for the collective use of arable and pasture land as well as machinery and tools. Type 3 finally is characterized by the collective use of *all* means of production including buildings. With all these variations any family is entitled to the use of up to 0·5 hectare of arable land and, in the third type, to keeping a limited number of cattle. Thus, with none of the three types is it a question of a total collectivization, in each case the farmers are able to use part of the means of production privately. Especially with fruit and vegetables private suppliers have a considerable share of the market. Collective ownership of land has not been juridically established, but private control is strictly limited.

While in 1960 the less strongly socialized collectives of types 1 and 2 made up a good third of the total, their share has been decreasing more and more in favour of the fully co-operative concerns of the third type. Today there are perhaps five times as many of the third type as of the other two. The reason for this was not coercive measures by the state, but rather the econo-

mic and social disadvantages which the more privately owned
collectives had to put up with, within the economic structure
of the GDR. Since the income of each collective depends both
on individual output and on its total productivity, the principle
of material interest works out in favour of economically efficient
structures. The total number of collectives is constantly dim-
inishing. Between 1960 and 1970 it decreased by half. Today there
are approximately 9000 collectives with an average size of 600
hectares of arable land. They can be regarded as large-scale
enterprises. For the purpose of further rationalization, the
collectives are combined in co-operative forms which also partly
include the foodstuffs industry and trade. Thus the agrarian
policy of the SED aspired to the second aim of its agrarian
reform after collectivization: the creation of efficient agricultural
units which are in a position to produce according to industrial
economic principles. In contrast to the transitional stage after
the agrarian reform, with its emphasis on collectivization, East
German agrarian policies today are concentrating wholly on the
creation of large-scale agricultural enterprises with specialized
production, aimed at achieving a sensible concentration of the
means of production and a rationalization of work processes.

The economic success of the restructuring of the agricultural
system compared with the unfavourable situation during the
1950s can be clearly seen from the statistics. Admittedly, in
comparison with western industrial states, there is still some
lagging behind, as in the industrial sector. The agricultural
productivity of the GDR (for instance the yield from the cultivated
area of wheat) still lags behind that of West Germany by about
15%. Work productivity too appears to be less in the GDR than
in the Federal Republic, despite the fact that the latter employs
fewer people in agriculture because it is incomparably better
mechanized. Yet as soon as it is no longer a question of yield
per hectare of grain or beet, but of human and social relationships
and activities, any comparison between the two systems becomes
virtually impossible. There is much to suggest that the social
and political effects of agricultural policies in the GDR may be
rated higher than the social effects of western agricultural policies.
The agrarian policies of the SED are concerned not only with
improving agricultural productivity and adapting agriculture
to an industrial society, but also perhaps to an even greater

F

extent with making its socio-political aims a reality. In this respect it has brought about fundamental changes which, all in all, may be regarded as positive, even from a western point of view.

The agrarian policies of the GDR have largely attempted to remove the traditional differences between town and country. The income of the members of the collectives is on average even a little higher than that of the population as a whole—not least thanks to the small entitlement to private ownership. Particularly in the field of education the traditional gap between town and country has been effectively overcome. More than half of those employed in agriculture have already gained some qualifications and the proportion of qualified specialist workers and graduates in the collectives is likely to increase still further. Those employed on the land in the GDR not only have the same opportunities for education and earnings, but they are also equally entitled to fixed hours of work, holidays, welfare and health services as the workers in the towns, which is certainly not true of many of the farmers in the West. The result is that East German citizens living in the country are by no means worse off than those in the towns; if anything they are rather better off. Those who at the end of the 1950s became members of collectives somewhat unwillingly, have now long been convinced that they owe a number of evident advantages to the agricultural policies of their state. If one compares the climate of relative contentment amongst the country population of the GDR with the constant complaints of farmers in the Common Market countries who see themselves as perpetual losers in an industrial society, then one can, at least in this respect, speak of the real and lasting success of the agricultural policies of the GDR.

This example shows what is also true elsewhere in East German society: the ruling minority carried out measures against the will of the majority of those affected, which after a certain time brought them social advantages which they would now no longer wish to give up. In this way the socialist agricultural system has become a factor in the economic and political stabilizing of the GDR régime.

7 THE COUNCIL FOR MUTUAL ECONOMIC AID (COMECON)

Within the political bloc under the leadership of the Soviet Union, the economy of the GDR is closely linked with the economic system of the socialist world. The institution giving expression to this international economic co-operation is the Council for Mutual Economic Aid, COMECON, founded in Warsaw in 1950. COMECON is only remotely comparable to the European Common Market. Whereas the Common Market is a supra-national organization with certain powers of its own, COMECON is simply a body co-ordinating the economies of the socialist bloc and intended to serve the 'international socialist division of labour'. Since they have no supra-national authority, the bodies of COMECON can only express recommendations to the individual governments but not themselves make binding decisions for their members.

Accordingly economic relationships between the socialist countries as a rule take the form of bilateral agreements. Of greatest importance for the GDR are the economic and trade agreements with the Soviet Union, for there the GDR sends the bulk of its exports and on the Soviet Union it depends for its most important raw materials. The Soviet Union, thanks to its enormous economic and political weight, is the leading member of the Council, followed by the GDR which has always striven to be a fully active and reliable member of COMECON.

A true integration of socialist economic territory under the umbrella of COMECON has so far not taken place, in spite of declarations to the contrary. This is due partly to the different degrees of development in the economies of the individual members of COMECON and partly to the defective international convertibility of the rouble as the main socialist currency. Thus the activities of the Council are concerned in the first place with the co-ordination of the national economic plans and with reaching agreement on the main aims of production, in order to work towards an economic plan embracing the whole of the socialist bloc. However, so far the co-ordination of plans has taken place mainly on the level of bilateral contacts and is far removed from any all-embracing economic plan for the bloc as a whole. At the last session of COMECON at Moscow in the summer of 1972 a renewed attempt was made to co-ordinate common economic relationships more intensively and to put common industrial projects into practice.

The last few years have shown that the growing importance of the East German economy for the eastern bloc has also strength-ened the political weight of the GDR within the alliance of socialist countries. It can be assumed that the efforts to achieve a rational division of labour in the communist economic bloc will be strengthened similarly to the capitalist countries, which have joined together to form more efficient, large-scale economic units as, for instance, in the extended Common Market.

1. Nawrocki J., *Zwanzig Jahre DDR-Wirtschaft* (Deutschland Archiv 1969), 952.

2. *Politische Oekonomie des Sozialismus und ihre Anwendung in der DDR* (East Berlin 1969), 177.

3. *Studien zur Geschichte der DDR in den sechziger Jahren* (Berlin 1971), 209.

4. Ulbricht, W., Foreword to *Politische Oekonomie,* op. cit., 9.

5. Immler, H., in Merkel, K. & Immler, H. (Eds.), *DDR-Landwirtschaft in der Diskussion* (Cologne 1972), 7.

9 | Foreign relations and defence policy

In its foreign policy as in every public and social sphere, the GDR represents a closed and harmonious system of aims and values. Whether the practical application of this system is equally consistent is a rather different matter. The GDR regards it as the main aim of its foreign policy to create favourable conditions internationally for the establishment of socialism. Since this is not simply in the national interest but concerns the whole of the socialist bloc, the foreign policy of the GDR—together with those socialist countries which recognize the leadership of the Soviet Union—is based on the principles of 'socialist internationalism'. In article 6 of its new Constitution, the GDR has expressly acknowledged the principles of socialist internationalism, and bound itself 'to cultivate and to develop co-operation and friendship in every sphere with the Union of Soviet Socialist Republics and the other socialist states'. These principles include 'brotherly co-operation' not only between the socialist states and especially with the Soviet Union, but also with the communist and workers' parties in non-socialist countries to support 'the struggle of national liberation movements against imperialism'. Relationships with states having different social orders are governed by the principle of 'peaceful coexistence' which the GDR interprets as establishing normal relations with the capitalist countries according to the rules of international law and thereby serving the cause of peace and *détente*.

From this main aim of socialist foreign policy—the creation of favourable international conditions for the establishment of socialism within the GDR and in the world—it naturally follows that there has to be a struggle against all political forces which work against these progressive principles of foreign policy and which, in the official terminology, are the embodiment of imperialism and reactionary forces. In Article 6 of its Constitution, which may be regarded as the general guideline for its foreign policy, the GDR declares itself to be pursuing a policy serving peace, socialism, international understanding and security. It further declares itself bound by the statutes of international law in so far as they serve peace and the peaceful co-operation between nations. In Article 8 of the Constitution it expressly pledges itself never to undertake a war of conquest nor to send its armed forces against any other free nation.

For a historically orientated theory of socialist foreign policies, 8 May 1945 may be seen as a turning point. In official writings that day, on which the unconditional surrender of Hitler's Germany was signed, is regarded as the day of national liberation for the German people. On that day, so it is asserted, a true 'national perspective' and a way into the community of nations was opened up for the German people. It heralded an upswing for the German nation to a better future, characterized by the fact that the German people (especially in the GDR) were bebeginning to free themselves from the grip of imperialism.

The second decisive turning point in this historical development is the date of the founding of the GDR (1949). From that date, so it is said, a completely new factor came into the system of international relations, namely the German workers' state. The newness is seen in the fact that, until then, the German state had been regarded purely as an imperialist and Fascist power, as a home of aggression and war, whereas now there was a German state within the international system which was pursuing a completely new path—the path of democracy, peace and friendship with all nations.

Seen from this ideological perspective, it was clear from the outset that the task of foreign policy of the GDR was to incorporate the state as firmly as possible into the group of states dominated by the Soviet Union. This was to be achieved very simply by a complete dependence on the foreign policies of the USSR. The other consequence was a strong concentration of foreign policy on the internal German struggle 'in order to bring about the final overthrow of German imperialism and militarism'.

2 RELATIONS WITH THE SOVIET UNION AND GERMAN POLICIES

Relations with the Soviet Union are thus fundamental to an understanding of the foreign policy of the GDR. Not only is the GDR, historically speaking, a creation of the Soviet power but as a sovereign state it is largely dependent on Soviet policies and even today it is to some degree—though less than before—an instrument of these policies. The reason given for the constantly emphasized common features in the foreign policy of both states is the 'indissoluble friendship' between them. The fact that there have been and indeed still are some conflicts of interest between the GDR and the Soviet Union is never admitted officially. However it can be shown that the interests of both countries were by no means always identical. The reasons behind the common foreign policy are stated as follows: 'The relationship between the GDR and the Soviet Union is based on the common ideas of socialist ideology, social order, their principal political and economic interests and above all on the friendly attitudes which permeate all levels of state, party and human relationships.'[1]

Seen historically, the relationship between the GDR and the Soviet Union has evolved in the following way: after the establishment of the GDR, the Soviet Military Administration was replaced by a Soviet Control Commission which was responsible for seeing that the Potsdam agreement and other decisions by the four powers regarding Germany were carried out: four years later it was transformed into a High Commission. The GDR itself dates its own responsibility for foreign policy back to the time of the establishment of the republic; however, it only received full sovereignty in matters of foreign policy on 25 March 1954 when the Soviet Union solemnly declared that it wished to establish the same relations with the GDR as with other sovereign states, although the Soviet Union still reserved for itself those functions arising out of the Four Power Agreement. In 1954 the High Commission was converted into a regular embassy.

The GDR interprets the granting of sovereignty by the Soviet Union as a consequence of the fact that within its own territories it had fulfilled all obligations imposed upon the whole of Germany in the Potsdam Agreement. The sovereignty of the GDR with regard to all questions of home and foreign policies, including relations with the Federal Republic, was ratified by international law in a treaty signed in September 1955 between the GDR and the Soviet Union. This treaty of 1955 was followed nine years later (in 1964) by a treaty of friendship which the GDR celebrates as being a particularly important event in the positive development of its foreign relations. This treaty of friendship with the Soviet Union is regarded as the legally effective expression of the close and brotherly relations between the two peoples and nations. In view of the distribution of power, the phrase 'brotherly relations' simply means that in all fundamental questions concerning its foreign policy, the GDR is bound by the aims of Soviet foreign policy and has always supported them. Since the Soviet policies concerning central Europe were directed primarily at safeguarding the results achieved by the Second World War and guaranteeing the territorial integrity of that area dominated by the Soviet Union, there was no fundamental conflict with the leadership of the GDR. However, the GDR was also compelled to associate itself with the various changes in the Soviet policy towards the West and the Federal Republic and occasionally submit to certain curtailments in its own full programme of foreign policies.

The establishment of the Federal Republic immediately followed by that of the GDR was the historical consequence of the struggle for power between the USA and the Soviet Union—which had emerged from the Second World War as super-powers—for the safeguarding and delimitation of their new spheres of influence. In the face of a further feared expansion of the Soviet sphere of influence, the Western powers regarded the division of Germany as inevitable. They were half-heartedly supported by the political parties and the people of West Germany and West Berlin who were more urgently concerned with keeping their traditional economic and social order and with re-establishing free and democratic institutions than with keeping national unity at any price. During the phase up to the establishment of the Federal Republic, German politicians in the Soviet zone of occupation massively supported all Soviet efforts to influence the shaping of Germany under the banner of German unity as a struggle against the 'dividers' of Germany. As is well known, the decisive steps leading to division—for instance the currency reform

of 1948—had been initiated by the western powers; the Soviet
Union carefully only took the corresponding steps within its
sphere at a later date. However, the policy of extensive political
co-ordination in the Soviet zone revealed to the western powers
and the West Germans at a very early stage exactly how the
Russians understood the carrying out of the Potsdam decisions
and their advocacy of the national unity of Germany.

When the division of Germany had been completed by the
establishment of two separate German states in 1949, there was
still a period of about six years in which the Russians, always
supported by their German representatives in East Berlin, attempted to prevent the full military integration of West Germany
and its economic potential into the western defence alliance of
NATO, founded in 1949. During this phase the Russians
even made tempting proposals for a reunification of Germany by
means of free elections. The first proposal of this kind was presented to the German *Bundestag* in 1951 by Otto Grotewohl,
Minister President of the GDR. It did indeed provide for German
reunification, which was of course the main aim in the West
German political programme, on the basis of all-German elections,
yet the GDR was not prepared to grant entry to a commission
from the United Nations which the western powers had invited
to visit both parts of Germany to investigate whether the holding
of really free elections could be guaranteed.

In March 1952 there then followed Stalin's famous Note to
the western powers in which he proposed the formation of an
all-German government, though without discussing in any detail
how this was actually to happen. The reunited Germany, to
which Stalin was prepared to allow an army of 100 000 soldiers,
was not to be permitted to join any alliance against any one of
the former victors—in other words it was to be militarily neutralized. Stalin's Note, which subsequently unleashed a heated
discussion in West Germany on the seriousness of its intentions,
was never thoroughly examined either by Adenauer or by the
western powers as to its concrete possibilities. Instead, trusting
in the 'policy of strength', West Germany's integration into the
western alliance was steadily pursued by signing the treaties of
Paris and Bonn. As long as these treaties had not yet been ratified
by the various parliaments, the Soviet Union in agreement with
the GDR still tried to prevent the ratification of the European

Defence Community Treaty. The rejection of the EDC Treaty by the French parliament in 1954 is therefore celebrated as a great victory for the Soviet and East German policies for peace in resisting the rebirth of German militarism. At the Berlin Conference on Germany which took place at the beginning of 1954 before the expected rejection of the EDC Treaty by France, no result was reached since the western powers insisted that a reunited Germany should be free to enter into an alliance, while the Soviet Union could not concede such a step since it would necessarily mean the removal of the GDR from its sphere of influence.

However, the decisive attempt of Soviet policy to prevent German rearmament was only temporarily successful. One year after the EDC proposals had come to naught, there followed the direct incorporation of the Federal Republic into NATO. Admittedly the Russians made one last attempt to hold up the military integration of West Germany by offering—together with the other socialist countries in the bloc—to discuss the creation of a collective security system in Europe. Yet, as the GDR maintains, 'all these warnings, all these offers to reach an understanding on the most urgent problems were ignored by the imperialist side'.[2]

The fact of West Germany's incorporation into the NATO alliance which was directed against the Soviet bloc, created a new situation for the foreign policies of the Soviet Union and the GDR. They responded to it by concluding the Warsaw Pact, a defence alliance of the socialist countries with united armed forces of all the participating nations under the command of the Soviet Union. Thereafter there was no more talk of any reunification of Germany in the foreign policy of the eastern bloc. The Summit Conference of 1955 held in Geneva to discuss the German problem came to grief already on matters of procedure.

From that time onwards, the Soviet and East German line on the German question has been unmistakable. The Soviet Union is no longer prepared to negotiate on the future of the GDR on the basis of any kind of reunification. Such negotiations have been made entirely the responsibility of the Germans themselves who alone are now considered to be competent to deal with questions of reunification and self-determination. Similarly the GDR has ceaselessly pointed to the factual existence of two

German states and declared that a reunification 'would only be possible on the basis of a *rapprochement* between the German Democratic Republic and the Federal Republic and taking full account of the interests of the GDR and its standing at home and abroad'.[3]

It is from this position that the GDR has, since 1955, been fighting an obstinate and finally even successful battle against the claim by the Federal Republic that it alone possessed the legal right to represent the interests of all German people (referred to by the GDR as 'arrogation of the sole right of representation'). Their battle has also been against the *Hallstein Doctrine* which provided that the Federal Republic would only maintain diplomatic relations with those countries which did not at the same time maintain such relations with the GDR. The only exception to this rule was the Soviet Union itself, with which the Federal Republic established diplomatic relations in 1955, because the Soviet Union was one of the four powers which had assumed responsibility for the whole of Germany by international law until the signing of a peace treaty. Meanwhile the resumption of diplomatic contacts between Bonn and Moscow has not solved any problems for West German reunification policies— quite the reverse. In the treaty of September 1955 between the GDR and the Soviet Union, the Soviet Union expressly transferred to the GDR free control over its relations with the Federal Republic, thus underlining its view that the question of German unity was a matter solely for the Germans themselves. Until 1973, however, the West Germans were not prepared to overcome the obstacle of the GDR's insistence on being recognized as a sovereign state.

In 1957, in the course of rethinking its policy for Germany, the GDR, through Grotewohl, suggested the creation of a confederation of the two German states but only on condition that the two states should previously leave their respective defence alliances and that the troops belonging to the four occupation powers should withdraw from Germany. Such suggestions had, on the one hand, a strongly rhetorical flavour and, on the other, produced the stereotyped West German reaction to strive for national reunification in peace and freedom on the basis of free elections. In any event the GDR no longer considered all-German elections to be appropriate after 1955 because it would be an illusion to try to bridge the differences between the two social systems by means of the ballot box. It defined its new policy towards West Germany as one of peaceful coexistence, being the progressive creation of conditions for living peacefully side by side on the basis of mutual recognition according to international law.

The aggressive policy of Khrushchev, introduced by the Berlin Ultimatum of 1958, which aimed at pushing the western powers out of Germany and turning Berlin into a demilitarized 'free city' and which, furthermore, had the intention of concluding a separate peace treaty with the GDR was strongly supported by its leadership. When, finally, his offensive failed with the American and Russian confrontation over Cuba, the GDR had to retreat also. The separate peace treaty was never concluded. From that time onwards the GDR has been concentrating on advancing its claim for recognition under international law and on using its growing economic strength in the Third World to help its efforts in this direction. Yet the breakthrough in the GDR's struggle for general international recognition only came in 1973 with Willy Brandt steering the *Ostpolitik* of the Federal Republic in the direction of greater normality.

3 THE WAY TOWARDS INTERNATIONAL RECOGNITION

The first increase in international estimation for the GDR came in 1959 with the Geneva Conference between the Foreign Ministers of the four powers responsible for Germany. This was the first time that delegations representing both German states were present at an international conference on Germany. Even though the German delegations did not possess full rights of participation and therefore sat at the side and not directly around the conference table, the GDR could nevertheless regard it as *de facto* recognition for itself. At Geneva negotiations for the re-establishment of German unity took place for the last time. Just as at earlier conferences, there could be no positive outcome, owing to irreconcilable positions of East and West.

The building of the Wall in August 1961, which initiated the inner consolidation of the GDR and against which the western powers dared do nothing, heralded a new phase in the foreign policy of the GDR. According to its own reports, the GDR could now continue its efforts to obtain recognition and to carry out its policy of peaceful coexistence 'under more favourable conditions and with greater peace and security'. On several occasions during the 1960s, the GDR suggested to the Federal Republic that more normal relations should be established between them, but always with the precondition of mutual recognition under international law, as a consequence of which the general recognition of the GDR would become possible. Despite its desire to alleviate human problems for the population, the Federal Republic would not assent to such a precondition. Thus from the outset it was the Federal Republic, together with the western powers, which proved to be the main obstacle to the GDR's desire for international recognition and right of representation in international organizations, especially UNO.

After 1961 certain arrangements between the two states became possible for the first time, at least below the level of official negotiations and settlements between the governments. Such arrangements included the agreement for the rebuilding of the motorway bridge over the Saale, the exchange of political prisoners and finally, too, the occasional agreements on passes between the Senate of West Berlin and the government of the GDR. An argument between the two German states over the question of an exchange of newspapers, as well as the discussion on an exchange of speakers between the SED and the SPD were dramatic but unfruitful interludes which contributed nothing to any *rapprochement*.

Meanwhile the position of the Federal Republic with regard to its avowed aim of German reunification had suffered some loss of credibility in West German public opinion and had also become uninteresting and indeed irksome to its western allies. While both the super-powers were making efforts to reach a *détente* between the blocs on the basis of the territorial *status quo* and thus continue the division of Germany, the traditional insistence of the Federal government on the 'four-power responsibility for the whole of Germany' proved to be politically unfruitful and of little constructive value. All this changed after the formation of the Grand Coalition when the SPD Foreign Minister, Willy Brandt, made a serious attempt in Bonn to give up outdated positions, to turn to a more realistic policy of renouncing power and to respect and even recognize the territorial *status quo* as regards the eastern bloc, thus opening up the way to a recognition of the GDR as a state. The western policy of *détente* and the new Bonn *Ostpolitik* had previously and temporarily raised hopes in eastern Europe of a certain easing of the European division between West and East, even before the important contractual agreements with the Soviet Union and with Poland in 1970. The most far-reaching and stirring expression of these hopes was the dramatic attempt by Czech communists to show a more human face of communism. This attempt at reform in Prague was suppressed by the Soviet allies of Czechoslovakia and included troops from the GDR using force of arms in the interests of the unity of the eastern bloc and not least in the interests of the GDR itself, which was seriously worried by the risk of 'infection' from developments in Czechoslovakia. Thus the *status quo* of division in Europe was strengthened anew by appealing to the Brezhnev doctrine of the priority of the interests of the socialist camp.

On this basis of power politics and with distinct differences of opinion with what it still considered as the 'imperialist' Federal Republic, the GDR, too, finally became more interested in making possible limited contractual agreements with the Federal Republic, using the principle of peaceful coexistence as a framework. Meetings took place between the Minister President of the GDR, Herr Stoph, and the Federal Chancellor Willy Brandt in Erfurt and Kassel in 1970, though without any tangible changes of attitude on either side. Because of Moscow's interest in normalizing the situation in Europe, the GDR even had to revise its long-held ideas of West Berlin as an 'independent political unit' and finally, willy-nilly, to submit to the so-called Berlin Agreement of 1972. This outcome of an agreement between the four powers was intended to stabilize the political position of Berlin for a long time to come. The GDR could expect limited settlements such as a traffic agreement with the Federal Republic or a general treaty on the relationship between the two German states (Basic Treaty), whilst awaiting international recognition by the Federal Republic and leading western states which would become a possibility in the near future. The treaty containing bases for relations between the Federal Republic and the German Democratic Republic was signed in the autumn of 1972 by the two negotiators, Herr Bahr for the Federal Republic and Herr Kohl for the GDR, and was ratified in the spring of 1973 by the *Bundestag* and the People's Chamber. It is the juridical basis for regular inter-governmental relations according to international law, but does not yet contain all formal consequences of legal recognition. The German states are represented in each case by accredited ministers and not by ambassadors. The treaty does not exclude any later decision by the two states in favour of reunification and expressly notes that the two signatories to the treaty hold differing views on this question. On the basis of this treaty, relations between the two countries are to return to normality and to be given a formal framework; moreover, it is intended to create the conditions for a series of intergovernmental agreements in the interests of the people 'on this side and that'. It also gives legal validity to the division of Germany which has existed *de facto* since 1949, but without making it irreversible. However, the unity of Germany cannot be re-established for the time being, neither in the original communist sense, namely by extending the 'progressive' socialist system to the whole of Germany, nor by joining the GDR to the Federal Republic in some way. 'The division of Germany will, in any event, last as long as there is a Soviet empire in Europe. And even if, one day, the Soviet presence in eastern Europe were to disappear under the threat of new problems, and the Germans in the GDR together with other East Europeans were to regain their freedom, the reunification of all Germans within one state would be by no means certain. For neither can it be foreseen whether people who have lived in two such radically different states could live together again in one social order—nor whether the neighbouring countries could, together with them, create a new European system which would be stable enough to integrate an undivided Germany effectively'.[4] The Basic Treaty heralds a new era in the relationship between the two states. The 'opposites' so characteristic of the era of the Cold War have become two nations existing side-by-side with the vague hope of an eventual 'togetherness'.

It is true that for many years ahead inter-German relations will still be difficult and characterized by mutual mistrust. The GDR especially fears that its people will be negatively influenced by greater contact with the West. It is extremely cautious in carrying out a policy of 'alleviating human problems' by which the Federal Republic sets particular store in the national interest. It faces the other Germany with a deliberate policy of ideological 'delimitation' towards the 'imperialist Federal Republic' in order to prove its political independence and its supposed historical role as a progressive German state.

In any event, in 1973 the GDR did achieve the principal goal of its foreign policy: since the autumn of 1973 the GDR, together with the Federal Republic, has been a member of UNO and meanwhile enjoys recognition by almost every country in the world including the western powers who had withheld it for so long because of their alliance with the Federal Republic. Until then the GDR had had only limited success in its difficult diplomatic battle for international recognition—mainly amongst those countries of the Third World not belonging to any bloc. However this world-wide recognition—greatly as it appears to crown the foreign policy of the GDR and the Soviet Union—also brings to an end the era of relatively international isolation and exposes the GDR more than ever to the critical appraisal of other states and to the necessity for international co-operation. This is a new state of affairs with which the GDR—especially in its relations with the Federal Republic—still has to come to terms. Yet little is likely to change in the near future as regards the close reliance of East German foreign policy on that of Moscow.

Compared with its relationship to the Soviet Union, relations between the GDR and the other countries of the Soviet bloc are of subordinate importance. Thanks to the leading role played by the Soviet Union, they are relatively free from tension though without being particularly close or friendly. Ever since its foundation the GDR has maintained diplomatic relations with all other countries of the eastern bloc and these were deepened during the second half of the 1950s on the model of relations with the Soviet Union by means of special treaties of friendship with Poland, Czechoslovakia, Hungary and Bulgaria. As early as 1950 in the Görlitz Agreement with Poland the GDR had declared the Oder–Neisse line as the 'inviolable frontier of peace and friendship' between the two states. Nevertheless, until 1971 when visas were no longer required before crossing the frontiers between the GDR, Poland and Czechoslovakia, these frontiers seemed hardly less hermetically sealed than those with the West.

In addition, as regards foreign and military policy, relations between the GDR and the other countries in eastern Europe dominated by the Soviet Union have been underpinned by economic agreements within the framework of the Council for Mutual Economic Aid (COMECON). The increase of economic power in the GDR has certainly also increased its political weight within the eastern bloc, which is not necessarily synonymous with greater standing amongst its socialist neighbours. Indeed, during the attempt at reform in Czechoslovakia, relations with this southern neighbour of the GDR were distinctly chilly. Nor did the GDR, faithful to its alliance, hesitate to take part in the occupation of Czechoslovakia by troops from Warsaw Pact countries, although the entry of a contingent from East Germany must have awakened terrible memories of the occupation of Czechoslovakia by Hitler's troops in 1939.

4 THE NATIONAL PEOPLE'S ARMY

The GDR possesses armed forces which are integrated into the military alliance of the Warsaw Pact. Their task is to protect and safeguard the socialist social order. 'Defending the attainments of socialism against any attacks from its enemies is a task of the socialist state, arising out of the deepest and most fundamental interests of the international working classes and of all peace-loving humanity.'[5]

The GDR maintains that—by creatively applying the Marxist-Leninist doctrine of defending the socialist fatherland—it has developed a military policy which reflects both the worldwide conflict between imperialism and socialism and the special conditions of class warfare against the reactionary political forces in the Federal Republic.[6] In fact the reason given for rearmament in the GDR has always been the acute military threat by its imperialist neighbour. Until the beginning of the 1970s both American imperialism and the ruling groups in West Germany thought to be allied to it were accused of having aggressive aims towards the GDR and the other socialist countries. Only the defensive power of the socialist coalition within the Warsaw Pact—so it was maintained—could put a stop to these aggressive plans. For all of twenty years the increasing efforts of the GDR to enlarge and modernize its defences have been motivated by

G

stereotyped arguments about growing dangers from western and particularly West German imperialism and militarism just as, conversely, the military policies of alliance between the western countries and West Germany have been similarly justified by reference to threats arising from the strong Soviet military power.

The core of the socialist defence forces of the GDR is the National People's Army but they also include the so-called border troops (which undertake to defend the state frontier) the state security service and the German People's Police is so far as the latter deal with matters of defence. Finally they include organizations concerned with civil defence, which however are not greatly developed, and also the 'action groups' of the SED in firms, official offices and all institutions dealing with defence training and education, the 'Society for Sport and Technology' being of special importance in this connection.

There are no official statistics about the numerical strength of the defence forces in the GDR, even less about its military equipment. If the border troops are counted as part of the East German army, which is quite justified since they come under the supreme command of the National People's Army, the total strength comes out at about 180 000. Of these almost a third are border troops; the strength of the army itself is estimated at about 85 000, the Air Force at 25 000 and the Navy at 15 000. The number of party members organized into action groups by the SED which should probably not be overestimated, lies around 300 000 to 400 000, while the number of members of the Society for Sport and Technology lies even somewhat above this figure. Altogether the total number of reservists who could be mobilized in a crisis is over 700 000.

The National People's Army developed from the People's Police who were quartered in barracks, and it has existed under its present name only since 1956, just a few months after the signing of the Warsaw Defence Pact. Just as in the Federal Republic where the younger generation has had little interest in the re-establishment of a national army, so too the East German leadership had no easy task in awakening any interest in matters of national defence amongst its young people during the years of building up first the People's Police and later the People's Army. It is noteworthy that general military service was not introduced until 1962, obviously because it was feared that its introduction would provide some of those affected with a good reason for emigrating. Before 1962 it was therefore one of the main tasks of the Youth Organization and especially the Society for Sport and Technology to mobilize young men who were willing to serve, although it was not always a case of 'voluntary' service. After the GDR had become a member of the Warsaw Pact, the People's Chamber passed an amendment to the Constitution in September 1955 which declared that service in defence of the country should be regarded as 'a national duty and honour'. However, general military service was not introduced by law until January 1962, half a year after the erection of the Berlin Wall. The 'Act concerning the Defence of the GDR' which forms the legal basis for the organization of national defence, was passed in September 1961.

Thus in the realm of military policies it was only the 'reliable defence of the national frontier' which created the required conditions for a more undisturbed development and a military improvement of the National People's Army. A message of greeting from the Central Committee of the SED and the Council of State on the occasion of the tenth anniversary of the People's Army in 1966 read as follows: 'The National People's Army has, during the past ten years, carried out its duties to the fatherland with honour. During this historically brief period our army has grown into an efficient and modern instrument of power in the first German workers' state. It is respected by our socialist comrades at arms, by the people of the socialist community and even by the patriotic forces in West Germany as being a reliable ally, and it is hated and feared by the enemies of the people.'

The army of the GDR was from the outset firmly integrated into the military organization of the Warsaw Pact. The leading military role of the Soviet Union is constantly emphasized in the official writings of the GDR, where it is maintained that developments in the Soviet Union set a standard for the creation and organization of defence in the other socialist states.

Soldiers in the GDR serve for 18 months. As a rule they are given a premilitary training by the Society for Sport and Technology. Because of the continual modernization of armaments, technological and practical training of soldiers has meanwhile become more important and has pushed the older methods of training which depended mainly on drill into the background.

The national leadership has concerned itself particularly intensively with the political education of the soldiers. For this special purpose so-called *Politoffiziere* (political officers) have been appointed and a large part of the training programme is given over to the political and ideological education of both officers and men. The main task of this ideological education is to convince the soldiers of the necessity of being absolutely prepared to defend the 'socialist fatherland of the workers'. In addition, the party itself is called upon persistently to deepen understanding amongst all the people for the necessity of defending socialist achievements. Until the time of East-West *détente* and the 'change through *rapprochement*' initiated by the Federal Republic, these ideas could be put across the more impressively, the blacker and more threatening were the pictures painted of renewed militarism and threatened dangers from West Germany. It was particularly important to encourage an awareness of the fact that military service and the defence of one's country in a socialist state and in a bourgeois-capitalist state differed fundamentally and that the revolutionary changes in social relationships brought about in the GDR must necessarily lead to a positive attitude to 'patriotic military service'.

Political work in the armed forces is the responsibility of both specially chosen leading cadres and party organizations within the forces themselves. Ideological work, over and above purely technical training is aimed at raising the troops' morale, effectiveness and willingness to fight. Whereas the reliability of army units before the building of the Berlin Wall was possibly not absolute everywhere, the consolidation of the state during the 1960s has increasingly raised the military value of East German troops within the framework of the Warsaw Pact. Today it is true to say that the National People's Army is no less a worthy partner in the Warsaw Pact than is the West German *Bundeswehr* within NATO.

For the National People's Army the problems of an inner constitution, the so-called 'inner structure', did not have the same significance as for the *Bundeswehr*. On the one hand there was, in the military sphere of the People's Army, no discussion at all regarding the traditional priorities of command and obedience; on the other, the military leadership of the GDR together with the ruling party tried again and again to convince both soldiers and citizens that military defence of a socialist state was not only a civic duty and honour but also that it was in no way connected with the reactionary phenomenon of militarism. In contrast to the Federal Republic with its fascist generals—so it was argued—the GDR was not threatened by 'militarism' at all. For these reasons purely outward national-military traditions (such as the old uniforms from the Third Reich army) could be restored more unconcernedly than in the West. On the other hand, the composition of the officer corps depended strictly on the correct selection of classes and ideological reliability. Only those officers from the former army were selected who had openly committed themselves to socialism, sometimes dating back to the days of the National Committee of Free Germany. Elsewhere consistent attempts were made to create a new type of officer having solidarity with the people. 80% of all officers of the National People's Army come from the working classes and 98% of all officers are also members of the SED, according to information given by the GDR. This makes it virtually impossible that the People's Army would ever deviate from the political direction set by the SED leadership. For this reason some military traditions, including the traditional Prussian goose-step used at official parades, are firmly incorporated into the prevailing political modes of behaviour of the socialist state. However, they no longer have any significance in themselves.

The relationship between officers and men has lost its element of social distance, formerly prevailing in Germany, because both groups are now subject to the new idea of 'socialist awareness'. There appears to be more democratization than in the old *Wehrmacht* or even in the present *Bundeswehr*. Certainly it would be inappropriate to characterize the National People's Army as a contemporary continuation of Prussian militarism or 'the spirit of army life' under a red flag. Despite some outward resemblances to the style and appearance of the old *Wehrmacht*, the GDR régime seems to have been more successful than that of the Federal Republic in creating an army which corresponds in its political awareness and its outward forms of behaviour to the special character of the political system which it is called upon to defend. In this way the leadership of the state controls a reliable military apparatus which cannot develop into a 'state within a state'. It seems equally true for the National People's

Army as for the *Bundeswehr* that—thanks to its firm integration into a military alliance—it cannot become an instrument of purely national interests and power-politics nor is it in a position to grasp a powerful political role for itself in the state.

1. Wünsche & Maretzki, 'Grundzüge der Aussenpolitik der DDR', in *Die DDR-Entwicklung, Aufbau and Zukunft, Marxist Blätter* (Frankfurt 1969), 52.

2. *Geschichte der Aussenpolitik der DDR* (Berlin-DDR 1968), 194.

3. ibid., 199.

4. Löwenthal, R., 'Europa und die deutsche Teilung', in Hofer, W., (Ed.), *Europa und die Einheit Deutschlands* (Cologne 1971), 329.

5. *Wissenschaftliche Entscheidungen-Historische Veränderungen-Fundamente der Zukunft,* Studien zur Geschichte der DDR in den sechziger Jahren (Berlin-DDR 1971).

6. ibid., 332.

10 | Two German states— one German nation?

As part of the policy of *détente* between East and West, both
German states are now in the process of normalizing their tense
relationship with each other and putting it on a formal basis
by legally binding agreements covering the whole (basic agreement)
and separate parts (part agreements). The two German states owe
their existence to the world-wide political confrontation between
East and West after the end of the Second World War. Within
the framework of the *détente* between the two power blocs which
began during the 1960s and was also strongly supported by the
Germans in the treaties of Moscow and Warsaw, the Federal
Republic and the GDR now have the task of transforming the
former confrontation into peaceful coexistence and co-operation.
To put it simply, they hope to 'develop normal neighbourly
relations with each other, such as are usual between states that
are independent of each other' (in the words of the agreement on
traffic between the Federal Republic and the GDR).

For many years an understanding between the states in the
sense of 'peaceful coexistence' was made impossible both on
account of the greater influence of the two super-powers involved
in the Cold War and on account of the differing policies of the
two German states. Only a world-wide *détente* on the basis of the
territorial *status quo* could prepare the way for an internal German
détente also. Admittedly the regularizing of such a relationship
is proving to be specially difficult and complicated, for that
between the Federal Republic and the GDR is burdened with the
legacy of years of defamation and obduracy which make it appear
impossible that the long-practised policies of militant opposition

should quickly be transformed into a policy of peaceful or even conciliatory togetherness.

This new policy for Germany with the aim of a well-ordered relationship of the two German states to one another has grown up out of the ruins of a reunification policy to which both sides paid lip-service until the last few years. Under the existing conditions and constellations of world politics, the reunification of a divided Germany into a new national state seems to be a Utopia which—even with a concentration of all the national energies of the Germans which at present appears unlikely—could hardly develop sufficient motive force to shift the rigid balance of power between East and West in Europe. In any event, the various ideas for reunification put forward by both sides were mutually unacceptable. Germans in the West understood reunification to mean principally the incorporation of East Germany into the political and social system of the Federal Republic, possibly coupled with certain reciprocal concessions; Germans in the East could only imagine the reunification of Germany as being an expansion of that democracy already existing in the GDR to the territory and people of the Federal Republic. The aim of an ultimate reunification has not been entirely dropped since this would run counter to the fundamental principle of national self-determination which both sides proclaim, but it does seem so far removed from all realistic policies that neither of the two governments is making any effort to embark on a concrete political path towards this goal. The time of plans for a united Germany is over.

After the years of bitter confrontation, both German states are now embarking on the difficult and certainly protracted process of internal German *détente* from which the thought of national reunification must for the time being be excluded. They do so on the basis of internal consolidation and their irreversible political and military integration on either side. They do so with the unalterable premise to which the Federal government has officially pledged itself, that there are two sovereign states on German soil and that the relationship between these states must develop on the basis of equality of rights and the binding force of agreements made between them. What is in dispute is whether there are two states made up from one German nation. On this question there are different viewpoints on either side of the Elbe (which is the northernmost boundary between the two German states). This question as to whether there is still a German nation might appear purely theoretical but it has political implications both for the concrete shaping of inter-German relations and also with regard to the distant aim of an ultimate amalgamation of the now divided parts of Germany. Today, therefore, the German question has become the question as to the continuance of the German nation.

2 THE EAST GERMAN VIEW OF THE GERMAN NATION

The Constitution of 1968 refers to the GDR as 'a socialist state of the German nation'. In its party programme of 1963, the SED still proceeded as a matter of course from the idea of the unity of the German nation and considered 'the safeguarding of the nation against war and destruction and the bringing about of a lasting peace as being the main problem of our time'. It pledged itself 'unshakeably' to re-establish the national unity of Germany and to overcome the division of Germany for which it blamed 'the imperialist western powers in league with West German monopolistic capitalism'. According to the SED programme, the battle for a uniform, democratic and peace-loving Germany had always been part of the good traditions of the revolutionary German workers' movement.

In the current jargon of the time, national unity required only the elimination of imperialists and militarists in West Germany. They would admittedly—so it was argued—speak hypocritically of national unity, but by their rejection of any understanding between the two states they were continually placing obstacles in the way of reunification. When, after 1969, the Federal government began to make its own contribution to world-politics and subsequently to inter-German *détente*, the political leadership of the GDR saw itself compelled to revise its ideas about a German nation. While previously it had spoken of a socialist state of the German nation, it has since 1970 referred to the GDR as a 'socialist German national state'. The GDR is thus the socialist German nation in contrast to the Federal Republic which it sees as a bourgeois German nation, while more recently still the description 'German' is omitted altogether in reference to the

Federal Republic. For what is important for the socialist GDR as a nation is not the historical reminiscence of nor even union with the German nation as a whole, but rather 'the increasingly closer co-operation and interaction with the other socialist nations'.[1] Socialist nations represent, historically speaking, a completely new type of nation and therefore it would only be possible to tackle those problems connected with the development of socialist nations by seeing them in the great international perspective and linking them with the world-wide battle between socialism and imperialism.[2]

Unmistakably the new line in GDR policies on the question of nationhood is the reaction to the policy of *détente* by the Federal government under Willy Brandt, which complies with the demand of the GDR for recognition, but still clings to the idea of the unity of the German nation—especially as this idea had been accepted by the GDR until 1969, though with a somewhat different political interpretation. Since then there has been silence on the question of a German nation in the GDR. The supposed continuance of the German nation, to which the Federal government attaches importance, is regarded by the GDR as 'nationalistic demagogy' being nothing but a renewed attempt 'at long last to put into practice the plans of diversion and expansion against the socialist GDR which have so far failed'.[3] However, history has already come to a decision on the unity of the German nation: it no longer exists. Instead, according to the present view of GDR ideology, there is on the one hand the bourgeois nation West Germany, characterized by class warfare, exploitation and aggression and, on the other, the socialist nation of East Germany, characterized by the planned development of productive forces and of all society on the basis of socialist production conditions and by a systematic propagation and process of socialist thought and action.

The aim of these arguments is clear. The GDR wishes to free itself from the common tie which the idea of a German nation still has for both states. Recently it has declared the concept of nationhood to be historically capable of change—like all social categories so too the concept of nationhood is not timeless nor independent of actual social conditions. Nowadays, it is argued, the nation is a product of the class struggle. After 1945 the class struggle in Germany led to the formation of two separate German nations, one socialist, one bourgeois. These two nations are the more sharply distinguished from each other since it is not the shared community of past history that is of importance but solely the attitude to class. Thus from the viewpoint of the GDR today there can no longer be any question of an undivided German nation in the sense of a common substratum underlying both German states.

3 THE WEST GERMAN VIEW OF THE GERMAN NATION

Because of the consistent repolarization of the idea of nationhood towards socialism, of which the formula of a socialist national East German state is the concrete expression, the GDR believes itself to have taken up the opposing position to the Federal government, which in its turn believes that the German nation still lives on despite the division of Germany into two states with differing social systems. The position taken by the Federal government on the question of the German nation was stated by the Federal Chancellor Willy Brandt on 14 January 1970 in his 'Report on the state of the nation in a divided Germany' as follows: '25 years after the unconditional surrender of the Hitler régime the concept of nationhood forms the bond holding the divided Germany together. In this concept historical reality and political will are united. Nationhood embraces and signifies more than a common language and culture, more than state and social order. A nation is founded on a lasting feeling of belonging together amongst its people. No one can deny that there is a German nation in this sense, and that it will continue for as far ahead as thought can reach. For the rest—also, or perhaps even, the GDR in its constitution admits to being a part of this German nation.'

The Federal government bases its claim to enter into a special kind of relationship with the GDR, which shall be binding in international law, on the thesis that the common bond of a German nation still lives on. Such an agreement would guarantee that neither West nor East Germany would consider each other as a foreign country. On this thesis of the continuance of a German nation, the Federal Government bases its political intention of promoting the cohesion of the nation by normalizing and formalizing the relationships between the two states, since it had been shown that the old policies of negation and non-recognition were threatening, more than ever before, to break the emotional bonds holding East and West together. On this same thesis, finally, the Federal government bases the whole aim of its policy for Germany, which is to shape inter-German relations in such a way as not to prevent a future reunification of the two separate parts.

4 DOES A GERMAN NATION STILL EXIST?

Theoretically this question seems to be the crux of the German problem. The Federal Republic answers it affirmatively and bases its policy of inter-German normalization on this premise. The GDR answers it negatively and bases its policy of delimitation as regards West Germany on the opposite premise of an at present insurmountable class division of the German nation into a bourgeois western and a socialist eastern part.

An answer to the question of the continuance of the German nation depends, of course, on the definition of 'nation'. Beginning with the famous formula by the French writer Renan that 'a nation is a daily renewable plebiscite' up to Friedrich Meinecke's well-known differentiation between a state-nation which coincides with national boundaries and a culture-nation which transcends state boundaries without being politically united, there are innumerable definitions, but without any academic consensus of opinion having so far been produced as to the correct one. If 'nation' really implies a daily plebiscite as Renan maintains, then it certainly cannot be proved in the case of the Germans whether they do still form a nation, for an open acknowledgement of political togetherness must be bound up with the actual conditions of the political system on this side as on that. Very few West Germans are at all interested in the possibility of a united Germany under a socialist banner; the political leadership of the GDR, on the other hand, declares that socialism alone is the essence of the true German nation and allows no scope for other expressions of the national will, even though they may exist in a latent form. If one uses Meinecke's distinction, it must be obvious that a uniform German state-nation certainly does not exist on account of its division, but that even the German cultural nation exists hardly at all or only very feebly because of the striking difference between the two social systems. If 'nation' is to have any meaning at all it must be understood as referring to a people moulded into a political unit or conscious of their political unity. In this context it is unimportant whether a people moulded by language, culture and history has to live under different political régimes, as is the case in Germany today, or not. One can speak of a nation if the people in their innermost hearts possess the political will towards national unity, or at least have a firm awareness of national togetherness, directed at a possible common life within one state. Using this criterion one can no longer speak with certainty of the existence of one nation in a divided Germany, but rather of one German people, living in two separate states.

The fact that the German people today have to live in two states with differing social systems naturally weakens national cohesion. The political elements which mould a people into a nation become practically effective in the two states in quite different ways. It is true that East and West Germans still possess strong rudimentary feelings of national togetherness and many, particularly the older generation, still have lasting memories of the historical community of the old German nation, but the shaping power of the political systems and the social surroundings created by them lead to a growing mutual estrangement of the population in the East and in the West. Thus there are in Germany today two peoples growing nationally ever further apart and becoming daily more different in their economic and social systems. The process of division has not only separated Germany into two states, it has even affected the German nation.

Whether, in the light of these facts, it is still possible to speak of a German nation or, what is more, make its continuance the basis of a policy has meanwhile become not only a question of fact but also a matter of will. For the potential continuance of a nation under the adverse circumstances of poltical separation depends decisively on whether one wishes to preserve the threatened unity of the nation or whether one is content to allow it to atrophy. If one were to abandon the idea of a German nation— in the sense of willing its political unity—completely, one would be proclaiming that the future restoration of national unity in Germany can no longer be a justifiable aim of German policy.

The Federal government is therefore acting correctly in attempting to bind the GDR to the previously used formula of a German nation, for only thus can special relations between the two German states be justified and only thus can reunification be maintained as a political—albeit far distant—aim. Yet the Bonn formula referring to two states from one German nation does not imply that the Germans are really a true nation in the political sense. They are, perhaps, a kind of 'remainder nation' though the remaining feeling of national togetherness seems strong enough on both sides to give the divided nation a new opportunity to bring about its political and thus its true national unity, should the constellation of world politics one day permit it.

The GDR may deny even more rigorously than before that there is such a remainder of the German nation; its constant references to the Federal Republic, its incessant boasts about its great political, economic and social achievements compared with West Germany, all reveal unintentionally to what extent East Germany has its eyes fixed on its western half. The reverse is much less true. This shows one tie, though mainly negative, between the GDR and the idea of a German nation. Here is this second German state wishing to be the better, more peace-loving and more democratic Germany having to prove itself day by day and pointing its finger at the other warped Germany in the West under the rod of imperialism. The GDR just like the Federal Republic is therefore quite incapable of withdrawing from the national cohesion produced by common history. Thus it remains the historical fate of a divided Germany that the states and their people will be unable to have a normal relationship with each other in the foreseeable future, even if 'completely normal relations' are established between them by international law.

The *détente* in the relations between the two German states, which has at last become possible through the *Ostpolitik* of the Brandt/Scheel government, is the serious attempt to preserve the remainder of a feeling of national togetherness amongst all Germans from further erosion by means of a policy of respect for given political realities. After the era of cherished illusions about one Germany only a policy based on a patient and realistic sense of proportion is in a position to guard and preserve that remaining feeling of national togetherness which is the indispensable requirement for a future restoration of German unity. For the rest we must free ourselves from the idea that a people can live happily only in one state. The twentieth century is in the course of developing new political forms beyond the traditional national state. It might well be that the German question may lose its political virulence and traditional problematic nature within the framework of an admittedly not yet discernible European peace. Yet before such possibilities appear, the Germany of the Federal Republic and the Germany of the GDR will have to find and, step by step, carve out a way of living with each other. A new chapter in German history has begun.

1. Hager, K., *Die entwickelte sozialistische Gesellschaft* (Berlin 1971), 55.

2. ibid.

3. ibid., 57.

Selected critical bibliography

The following bibliography attempts to clarify the problem of political attitudes, found in studies of the GDR, by means of brief comments which, of course, also reflect subjective values and opinions. Under each chapter heading may be found first English language titles, then publications from the GDR and finally from the Federal Republic. The publications from the GDR are indispensable both as a source for the national consciousness of the GDR, and as documents of contemporary historical development; for this reason all further research on the GDR really requires a knowledge of German. We have only included very few West German publications as important or supplementary material: further references may be found in the German edition of this book (Hamburg, 1972).

A detailed though not the most recent bibliography is contained in: Paul L. Horecky (Ed.), *East Central Europe: a Guide to Basic Publications* (Chicago & London 1969) part 3, *East Germany*, 361–440. In this volume Melvin Croan has given a very competent commentary on those publications dealing with politics and society.

We have marked with an asterisk those books which we consider to be most important for introductory reading and for the present state of research.

General

Childs, David, *East Germany* (London and New York 1969). An all-round portrayal of the political system of the GDR which emphasizes the development of the SED, its composition and methods of government from 1963. Makes a useful comparison between the two Constitutions of 1949 and gives an account of the educational system. It may be criticized for taking the self-portrayal of the GDR too much at face value. Cf. the instructive review by Peter C. Ludz, 'Discovery and "Recognition" of East Germany', *Comparative Politics,* vol. 2 (1969–70), 681–92.

Dornberg, John, *The Other Germany* (Garden City, New York 1968). Dornberg's own impressions and conversations form the basis of his book on the political and social everyday life of the GDR.

*Hanhardt, Arthur M., Jr, *The German Democratic Republic* (Baltimore 1968). A brief and very useful introduction to the socio-political development of the GDR. It takes account of changes in the economy and in political culture and deals particularly with the function of the GDR in the integration of eastern Europe.

*Ludz, Peter Christian, 'The German Democratic Republic from the sixties to the seventies', *Occasional Papers in International Affairs*, no. 26. (Harvard 1970). A 'socio-political analysis' of trends in the development of the GDR.

*Smith, Jean Edward, *Germany beyond the Wall: People, Politics and Prosperity* (Boston and Toronto 1969). This book, the first socio-political all-round portrayal of the GDR published in the USA, is still very useful today, especially in its description and analysis of everyday life in the GDR. Has an English translation of the East German Constitution of 1968 (245–72).

Doernberg, Stefan, *Kurze Geschichte der DDR* (Berlin-DDR 1969). An official history of the GDR by the director of the Institute for Contemporary History in East Berlin.

A bis Z. A pocket reference book on the other part of Germany, published by the Federal Ministry for Intra-German Affairs (11th ed., Bonn 1969).

Periodicals

English-language articles in learned journals may be found, if at all, in the two following:

Problems of Communism, now in its 23rd year (1974).

Survey. A journal on East and West Studies, now in its 20th year (1974).

Neues Deutschland, now in its 28th year (1973). The 'organ of the Central Committee of the SED', published daily and the most important newspaper of the GDR.

Einheit, now in its 28th year (1973). This 'Journal for the theory and practice of academic socialism' is also published by the Central Committee of the SED and is an important source for the political and social discussion of the GDR and its development.

Deutschland Archiv, now in its 6th year (1973). The most important West German 'Journal for East German affairs and intra-German policies'.

1. The division of Germany and the birth of the GDR

Balfour, Michael & Mair, John, *Four-Power Control in Germany and Austria* (London, New York and Toronto 1956). Still the standard work for the contemporary history of Germany between May 1945 and December 1946.

*Baring, Arnulf, *Uprising in East Germany: June 17 1953* (Ithaca and London 1972). An informative analytical study on the background, course and consequences of the East German revolt of June 1953. (The preface by Richard Loewenthal sketches the general political background).

Leonhard, Wolfgang, *Child of the Revolution* (Chicago 1958). The account [by a former communist youth leader who came to Berlin from Moscow with Ulbricht in 1945] of the beginnings of the sovietization of East Germany.

*Nettl, John P., *The Eastern Zone and Soviet Policy in Germany 1945–50* (Oxford Univ. Press 1951). A very useful survey of the Soviet era of occupation and especially of the rebuilding of administration and the economy.

Badstübner, Rolf & Thomas, Siegfried, *Die Spaltung Deutschlands 1945–1949* (Berlin-DDR 1966). These two East German historians lay the blame for the division of Germany on the West Germans and the western allies.

Geschichte der deutschen Arbeiterbewegung, 8 vols. (Berlin-DDR 1966). In this History of the German Workers' Movement, published for the Institute for Marxism and Leninism by the Central Committee of the SED, volumes 6, 7 and 8 deal with the history of the GDR from 1945 to the beginning of 1963.

*Weber, Hermann, *Von der SBZ zur DDR. 1945–1968* (Hannover 1968).

2. The interpretation of ideology and social reality in the GDR

Havemann, Robert, *Questions, answers, questions; from the biography of a German Marxist* (Garden City, New York 1972). Havemann's unorthodox ideas are typical of the supporters of a 'third way', a kind of free socialism.

Ulbricht, Walter, 'On questions of socialist construction of the GDR'. From *Speeches and Essays* (Dresden 1968).

Hager, Kurt, *Die entwickelte sozialistische Gesellschaft* (Berlin-DDR 1971). The Central Committee's Secretary for Ideology gives the official interpretation of the GDR and its problems as a 'developed socialist society'.

Kleines Politisches Wörterbuch (Berlin-DDR 1973). The quickest way to obtain information about the official interpretation of the GDR on political and social matters.

Rudolph, Hermann, *Die Gesellschaft der DDR—eine deutsche Möglichkeit?* (Munich 1972). A stimulating essay on the tensions between official interpretations and actual National Consciousness in the GDR.

3. The SED and the National Front

*Ludz, Peter Christian, *The changing party in East Germany* (Cambridge, Mass. 1972). Ludz sees a transition from totalitarianism to 'consultative authoritarianism' in the GDR through changes in the structure of the party and its methods of government.

Stern, Carola, *Ulbricht: A Political Biography* (New York 1965). An excellent and critical political biography of Ulbricht. It is also the best introduction to the internal party arguments of the SED up to 1963.

Dokumente der Sozialistischen Einheitspartei Deutschlands (Berlin-DDR, 1950 ff., at present 13 vols). An indispensable primary source.

Weber, Hermann & Oldenburg, Fred, *25 Jahre SED* (2nd ed. Cologne 1971). A chronology of the history of the SED.

4. The structure of the state

Bothe, Michael, 'The 1968 Constitution of East Germany', *American Journal of Comparative Law*, vol. 17 (1969), 268–91. A survey of the GDR Constitution of 1968 which sees it as a codification of Marxist-Leninist ideals on state and government.

Das System der sozialistischen Gesellschafts- und Staatsordnung in der Deutschen Demokratischen Republik (Berlin-DDR 1970). Includes the SED manifesto of 1963, the Constitution of 1968 and extracts from important laws and decrees.

Handbuch der Volkskammer der Deutschen Demokratischen Republik, currently for the 5th electoral period (Berlin-DDR 1972).

Staat und Recht. This journal, published by the Academy for Political Science and Jurisprudence, is the most important East German publication on matters of public law.

Sorgenicht, Klaus, *et al* (Eds.), *Verfassung der Deutschen Demokratischen Republik* (Berlin-DDR 1969). The official commentary on the Constitution of 1968.

Mampel, Siegfried, *Die sozialistische Verfassung der Deutschen Demokratischen Republik* (Frankfurt 1972). A comparison of Constitutional Law with constitutional reality in the GDR.

5. The legal system

*Kirchheimer, Otto, *Political Justice* (Princeton, New Jersey 1961) chapter 'Democratic centralism and political integration of the judiciary', 259–303.

Markowits, Inga S., 'Civil Law in East Germany: its Development and Relation to Soviet Legal History and Ideology', *Yale Law Journal*, vol. 78 (1968/69), 1–51.

Weiss, Edith Brown, 'The East German Social Courts: Development and Comparison with China', *American Journal of Comparative Law*, vol. 20 (1972), 266–89.

Neue Justiz. Journal for Law and Jurisprudence, published by the Supreme Court of the GDR.

**Kleines Wörterbuch der marxistisch-leninistischen Staats- und Rechtstheorie* (Berlin-DDR 1973). This dictionary is published by the East German Academy for Political Science and Jurisprudence in Potsdam-Babelsberg and gives the official attitude on all matters of political and legal theory.

6. Social structure and social policies

*Ludz, Peter Christian, *The German Democratic Republic from the sixties to the seventies* (Cambridge, Mass. 1970).

Solberg, R. W., *God and Caesar in East Germany. The Conflicts of Church and State in East Germany since 1945* (New York 1961).

Statistical Pocket Book of the German Democratic Republic. Published by the State Central Administration of Statistics (Berlin-DDR 1959 onwards). Tables are extracted from the *Statistisches Jahrbuch der DDR*.

Statistisches Jahrbuch der Deutschen Demokratischen Republik, Staatliche Zentralverwaltung für Statistik, (Eds.) annually since 1956, (Berlin-DDR).

*Einhorn, Wolfgang *et al* (Eds.), *Wörterbuch der Marxistisch-Leninistischen Soziologie* (Berlin-DDR 1969). Encyclopaedic articles on all matters of social theory and practice in the GDR.

Ludz, Peter Christian, (Ed.), 'Studien und Materialien zur Soziologie der DDR' (special issue, 1964 of the *Kölner Zeitschrift für Soziologie und Sozialpsychologie*) (Cologne and Opladen 1964).

Materialien zum Bericht zur Lage der Nation 1971 (Opladen 1971). This compilation of empirical and statistical data was produced by a team of scholars on behalf of the government of the Federal Republic. It gives statistical comparisons between the Federal Republic and the GDR in different spheres of life such as production and consumption, the health and welfare systems and the role of women and young people.

Storbeck, Dietrich, *Soziale Strukturen in Mitteldeutschland* (Berlin 1964). A sociological and statistical analysis of the population and of social and economic structures in the GDR, including many comparisons with the Federal Republic.

7. The educational system

*Hanhardt, Arthur M., Jr, 'Political Socialization in the German Democratic Republic, *Societas. A Review for Social History*, vol. 1, no. 2 (Spring 1971) 101–21. The institutions of the educational system and what they teach are analysed to show their function in the education of 'socialist personalities'.

Gesetz über das einheitliche Bildungssystem der DDR (vom 25. Februar 1965) (Berlin-DDR 1971 and onwards). The fundamental Act dealing with the educational system.

Günther, Karl-Heinz & Uhlig, Gottfried, *Geschichte der Schule in der Deutschen Demokratischen Republik 1945 bis 1968* (Berlin-DDR 1970). The development of school and educational policies from 1945, written by two leading educationalists.

Baske, Siegfried & Engelbert, Martha (Eds.), *Zwei Jahrzehnte Bildungspolitik in der Sowjetzone Deutschlands* (2 vols., Heidelberg 1966). This collection of documents, including the Education Act of 1965, depicts the development of East German educational policies from 1945. Has a very useful introduction.

*Siebert, Horst, *Bildungspraxis in Deutschland* (Düsseldorf 1970). A brief and informative comparison of the educational institutions in the two German states, with special reference to schools and adult education.

8. The economic system

*Pounds, Norman J. G., *Eastern Europe* (Chicago 1969). Its chapter on the GDR gives a very good economic and geographical description of East Germany. Useful references to further specialized literature.

Schnitzer, Martin, *East and West Germany: A Comparative Analysis* (New York, Washington and London 1972). Schnitzer compares

the economies of the Federal Republic and the GDR. He confines himself mainly to the comparison of statistics and bases his hypotheses on a rigid model where capitalist economy = free
planned economy = not free.

Stolper, Wolfgang F., with the assistance of Karl W. Roskamp, *The Structure of the East German Economy* (Cambridge, Mass. 1960). Somewhat out of date in material, but is still indispensable for understanding the economic development of the GDR after the Second World War—e.g. in the effect of reparations. It is distinguished by its astonishing wealth of information and methodological precision.

Müller, Hans & Reissig, Karl, *Wirtschaftswunder DDR* (Berlin-DDR 1968). The official economic history of the GDR for the years from 1945 to 1967.

Politische Ökonomie des Sozialismus und ihre Anwendung in der DDR (Berlin-DDR 1969). The standard work on the interpretation of the GDR as a socialist economic system.

*Wörterbuch der Ökonomie/Sozialismus (3rd ed. Berlin-DDR 1973). The new edition of this encyclopaedia on socialist economic theory and practice presents the economic doctrines at present prevailing in the GDR.

*Mitscherling, Peter *et al*, *DDR-Wirtschaft. Eine Bestandaufnahme* (Frankfurt 1971). The best documented presentation in statistical terms of all spheres of the East German economy, by a team of collaborators from the German Institute for Economic Research in West Berlin.

9. Foreign relations and defence policy

Sinanian, S., Deak, I., Lutz, P.C. (Eds.), *Eastern Europe in the 1970s* (New York, Washington and London 1972).

Forster, Thomas Manfred, *The East German Army; a pattern of a communist military establishment* (London 1967).

Stern, Carola, 'East Germany', in William E. Griffith (Ed.), *Communism in Europe. Continuity, Change and the Sino-Soviet Dispute* (Cambridge, Mass. 1966), vol. 2, 43–154. A very well-informed summary of the home and foreign policies of the SED up to 1965.

Deutsche Aussenpolitik. The official East German journal on matters of foreign policy, published by the Academy for Political Science and Jurisprudence.

Dokumente zur Aussenpolitik der Deutschen Demokratischen Republik, vols. 1–19 (Berlin-DDR 1954–73). These annual volumes contain the official documents on the foreign policy of the GDR.

Hänisch, Werner, *Aussenpolitik und internationale Beziehungen der DDR,* vol. 1 1949–1955 (Berlin-DDR 1972). The author of this history of the foreign policy of the GDR is the Director of the Institute of International Relations at the Academy for Political Science and Jurisprudence.

Winzer, Otto, *Deutsche Aussenpolitik des Friedens und des Sozialismus* (Berlin-DDR 1968). Policy programme of the present Foreign Minister of the GDR, in office since 1965.

Dasbach-Mallinckrodt, Anita, *Wer macht die Aussenpolitik der DDR?* (Düsseldorf 1972). A well documented presentation and analysis of the apparatus, the aims and the methods of East German foreign policy.

10. Two German states—one German nation?

Hartmann, Frederic H., *Germany between East and West: the Reunification Problem* (Englewood Cliffs 1965). Restricts itself to diplomatic history and conferences without discussing the internal political aspects.

Ulbricht, Walter, *Whither Germany?* (Dresden 1966). Ulbricht's 'Speeches and Essays on the National Question', from the years 1930 to 1966.

Vali, Ferenc A., *The Quest for a United Germany* (Baltimore 1967). This book portrays the origins, developments and suggested solutions of the 'German question' from a western standpoint. It does not do justice to the internal development of the GDR.

Windsor, Philip, *German Reunification* (London 1969). A stimulating essay on the strategic, world political background to the German problem, showing the transformation of the GDR from a satellite to a junior partner of the Soviet Union.

Norden, Albrecht & Matern, Hermann & Ebert, Friedrich, *Zwei deutsche Staaten. Die nationale Politik der DDR* (Vienna 1967). The national question and its suggested solutions from the East German standpoint, written by three prominent functionaries of the SED.

Bender, Peter, *Zehn Gründe für die Anerkennung der DDR* (Frankfurt 1968). Presents the arguments for the recognition of the GDR as being a precondition for the political 'liberalization' of East Germany.

Index